Richard Hammond

Can you feel the
FORCE?

DK Publishing, Inc.

LONDON, NEW YORK, MUNICH,
MELBOURNE, and DELHI

Senior editor Ben Morgan
Designed by Leah Germann, Clare Harris,
Karen Hood, Claire Patané
Design assistant Gemma Fletcher
DTP designer Almudena Díaz
Production Seyhan Esen-Yagmurlu
US editor Margaret Parrish
Jacket designer Hedi Gutt
Jacket editor Mariza O'Keeffe
Jacket copywriter Adam Powley

Publishing manager Susan Leonard

Consultants Dr. Jon Woodcock, Chris Woodford

First American Edition, 2006
Published in the United States by
DK Publishing, Inc., 375 Hudson Street
New York, New York 10014

06 07 08 09 10 10 9 8 7 6 5 4 3 2 1

Library of Congress Cataloging-in-Publication Data

Hammond, Richard, 1969-
Can you feel the force? / written by Richard Hammond. -- 1st American ed.
p. cm. Includes index.
ISBN-13: 978-0-7566-2033-2
ISBN-10: 0-7566-2033-3
1. Physics--Popular works. 2. Force and energy--Popular works. I. Title.
QC24.5.H357 2006
530--dc22
2006016429

Color reproduction by Icon Reproductions, London
Printed and bound by Toppan in China

Discover more at
www.dk.com

It's no secret that I love cars—and bikes, and planes, and speedboats, and hovercraft and, well, anything that moves really. And the reason I love them? Because they're all about action—stuff happening. When I drive a car round a racetrack, I can feel things going on all around me: the tires scrabbling for grip, the acceleration pushing me back in the seat, the seatbelt straining when I hit the brakes and fly forward. In other words, there are a whole lot of forces going on. And that's physics.

Physics is the action department of science. When a car crashes, an apple falls out of a tree, or lightning strikes, the laws of physics can tell you what's going on. Biology and chemistry might be able to tell you why an apple tastes the way it does, but only physics can explain what happens if you throw it at a brick wall at 200 mph (320 km/h).

Of course, it's not all fast cars and squashed apples. In fact, physics is about, well, *everything*— from the inconceivably tiny bits of stuff the universe is made of to the inconceivable vastness of the universe itself. Physics is also the weird end of science. It's about the invisible, the unexplained, and the downright strange. Think of the slippery force that pushes magnets apart when you try to press two north poles together. What *is* that force and why is it there?

You might think scientists have got everything worked out, but the truth is that science is full of mysteries and questions, and that's why this book is full of questions too. Most of them have easy answers, but some have no answer yet. Some might surprise you, others might shock, and some are there just to make you think... We hope you enjoy them.

RICHARD HAMMOND

CONTENTS

"People have been using physics since ... well, since people began.

It came in very handy for pushing mammoths off cliffs, lighting fires, throwing spears, and pushing more mammoths off cliffs. So we human beings have always been pretty good at using physics.

But we weren't so good at understanding why things worked the way they did.

Why did a spear fly in a curve when we threw it? How did fire burn our hands and cook our food? And why did the mammoth fall off the cliff? We only really began to find answers when we started doing experiments and measuring things. *And to understand how that got going, we have to travel back in time about 3,000 years ...* "

In the beginning

Greece is the *word*

Since the dawn of time, people relied on superstitions and *myths* to explain how the world works. But about 3,000 years ago, in Greece, things changed. People stopped trusting their ancient beliefs and decided to think everything through from scratch. It was almost the beginning of science (but not quite).

Amber

AMAZING AMBER

The Greeks were philosophers (thinkers) rather than true scientists—they had great ideas, but they rarely conducted experiments to check them. Even so, they did make scientific discoveries. They'd discovered **static electricity** by 600 BC. They knew that rubbing amber (a kind of stone) with wool made it pull feathers as if by magic.

The word "electricity" comes from *elektron,* the Greek for amber

600 BC

400 BC

MAGNETIC SOLES

According to legend, a Greek shepherd called Magnes discovered the force of **magnetism** when his feet stuck to a mountain, the iron nails in his sandals pulled by a magnetic rock called lodestone. The Greeks thought lodestone contained a "soul" that pulled iron toward it.

WHAT'S THE MATTER?

The Greeks came up with the theory that everything is made of **atoms**—particles so tiny that nothing could be smaller. They had no evidence for this bold theory, it was really just a lucky guess. They thought the shapes of atoms might explain their properties, so they gave fire sharp, spiky atoms and made water atoms more rounded.

Fire

Water

Air

Earth

Why *do* elephants FALL faster?

Aristotle

Like many great thinkers and scientists, Aristotle was a little eccentric. He spoke with a fake lisp, which he thought was sophisticated, and he was very fussy about his clothes and hairstyle. He wasn't especially good at physics, but because he was brilliant at most other subjects, his ideas held sway for centuries.

ARISTOTLE
384–322 BC

FEATHER DOWN

One of the first people to think about **gravity** was a Greek philosopher named Aristotle. Aristotle noticed that bricks fall faster than feathers and concluded (without checking) that the heavier something is, the faster it must fall. He was wrong, but nobody conducted an experiment to check the theory until nearly 2,000 years later.

350 BC

KEEP ON MOVING

Aristotle tried to explain how **forces** makes things move. He thought a moving object must always have a force pushing it, but he was wrong again. In fact, an object can keep moving forever without a force, but **friction** usually slows everything down.

EUREKA!

The smartest of the Greeks was a man named Archimedes, who once leapt out of his bath and ran **naked** down the street shrieking "Eureka!" after solving a puzzle. The king had asked him to examine a new crown and find out, without cutting it, if it was made of solid gold. The solution came to Archimedes in the bathtub. He could measure the crown's **volume** by placing it in water and seeing how much the level rose. If an equal weight of gold had the same volume, the crown must be real. As it turned out, the crown was fake and the goldsmith was executed.

IN THE MIDDLE

Most people used to think Earth was flat, but the bright Greeks not only realized Earth is round, but figured out its size by measuring shadows in different places. But they didn't know Earth is *turning*, so they naturally thought the Sun and stars cross the sky because they're moving around us. Because they got this wrong, the Greeks thought Earth was the **middle of the universe**, and this idea stuck for many centuries.

250 BC   240 BC

WEAPONS OF WAR

Archimedes was a brilliant inventor. He figured out how levers magnify forces, and then used the principle of the lever to build war machines for fighting the Romans. One was an enormous wooden crane with a hook dangling from a rope. It could pick up ships just offshore and roll them over or smash them on the rocks, killing everyone on board.

With a long enough lever I can lift anything!

ARCHIMEDES
287–212 BC

According to
Greek legends,
a god called
Atlas held up
the universe

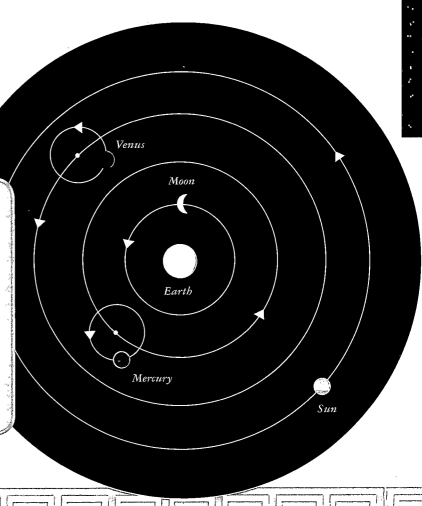

Venus

Moon

Earth

Mercury

Sun

HEAVENLY SPHERES

Since the Sun, stars, and planets seemed to go around the Earth, the Greeks thought the universe was based on circles. They thought each planet was attached to a gigantic glass sphere that revolved around the Earth, with the stars all on one whopping great sphere outside the planets. The Greeks found that they could use this theory to predict where planets would rise and fall, though they had to add fiddly little spheres to the large spheres to make it work. In fact, it worked so well that people continued to believe in it for nearly 2,000 years.

150 BC   50 AD

GREEK GEEK

One of the last of the Greek philosophers was an inventor called Hero. He built all kinds of strange contraptions, including mechanical birds that sang, a mileometer for chariots, a machine gun, and the world's first coin-operated vending machine. Hero realized that air is a substance and discovered he could compress it. This led him to believe that it must be made of atoms.

were all stuck to colossal glass balls

The DARK AGES

After the Greek era ended, people turned back to myths, magic, and religion. For more than a thousand years, superstition ruled the world, except for a few glimmerings of scientific progress....

500 AD

700 AD

IT'S A KIND OF MAGIC

The apparently magical abilities of **magnets** led to all kinds of myths in the Dark Ages. People thought a magnet held to the head would cure a person of sadness. They thought garlic and diamonds destroyed the power of magnets and that dipping a magnet in fresh goat's blood restored it to full strength.

POINTING THE WAY

While Europeans were busy rubbing their magnets with garlic and blood, the Chinese were rubbing theirs with iron needles, which became magnetic too. When one of these needles was hung on a thread, it pointed north. The Chinese had invented the pocket compass.

The knowledge of the ancient Greeks was preserved by the Arabs

SUN

LIGHT RAYS

Peregrinus found that magnets can push as well as pull

1000 AD

1300 AD

SEEING THE LIGHT

The teachings of ancient Greece were lost from Europe but preserved in the Arab world, where the spirit of science survived. The Greeks had thought we see because our eyes emit invisible rays that bounce back. In 1000 AD, an Egyptian called Alhazen realized the truth: light from the Sun or flames bounces off objects and only then enters our eyes.

POLES APART

Back in Europe, a Frenchman, Peregrinus, tried to separate the north and south poles of magnets by snapping them. He found, to his amazement, that each half always became a complete magnet with its own two poles, no matter how many times he divided it.

Late Chinese compass

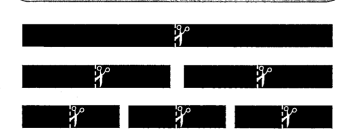

Into *the light*

About 500 years ago

in Europe, there was an amazing change in the way people thought. As in ancient Greece, people began to question their old religious and superstitious ideas about the world, but this time they did something else too. They did **experiments** to test which ideas were right. It was the beginning of science, and it changed the world forever.

Nicolas Copernicus
(1473–1543)

1507

A BRILLIANT IDEA

Since Greek times, people had thought the Earth sits motionless in the middle of the universe, with the Sun and planets all whirling around us. In 1507, a Polish astronomer named Nicolas Copernicus noticed it was much easier to predict the motions of planets if you supposed the Sun was in the middle with Earth traveling around it, rather than vice versa. When other astronomers put Copernicus's theory to the test, it worked well. But there was a big problem ...

14 Could the *whole world* really be spinning?

Copernicus put the Sun in the middle of his model of the universe, even though it meant that Earth must be flying through space.

Mars

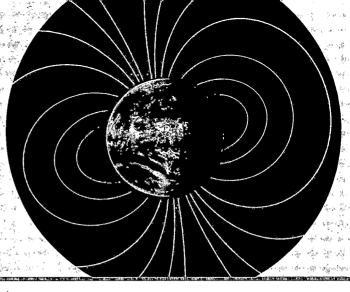

THE WAY SCIENCE WORKS

The difference between science and other ways of thinking is that scientists conduct experiments to check if a theory (an idea) is right. William Gilbert of England was the first person to study magnets scientifically. Instead of simply accepting the old story about garlic ruining magnets, he rubbled garlic on magnets and tested them—it made no difference. Gilbert also noticed that magnetic needles point slightly into the ground and formed a theory that Earth is a magnet. He was right.

1543

1580

A DANGEROUS IDEA

Religious people hated Copernicus's idea because they believed God created the universe with Earth in the middle. Copernicus put the theory in a book but, afraid of offending the Church, waited until he was on his deathbed before publishing it; he also added a flattering dedication to the pope.

A CRAZY IDEA?

There was another reason Copernicus's idea was hard to believe. If it was true, it meant that the Sun's motion across the sky was just an illusion caused by Earth spinning around at ferocious speed. People thought that was impossible. If Earth was spinning, they thought, birds and clouds would be left behind and buildings would fall over. This puzzle was solved by the next person in our story ...

Galileo's WORLD

The world's *first modern scientist* was an Italian named Galileo. His ingenious experiments showed that the Greeks hadn't just been wrong about space—they were wrong about gravity and motion, too. Galileo's discoveries were the start of physics, but they got him into *deep trouble*.

Leaning Tower of Pisa

TOGETHER WE FALL

Legend has it that Galileo dropped balls of different weight off the Leaning Tower of Pisa to show they hit the ground together. In fact, he probably just rolled balls down ramps, but it's true he disproved the old Greek idea that heavy objects fall proportionately faster than light ones. As Galileo found, all objects are pulled down by gravity at the same rate, unless they are so light or fluffy that the air can slow them down.

This is where physics REALLY *starts!*

1590

Galileo figured out the precise curve of a ball in flight by separating it into two parts: a constant horizontal speed and a changing vertical speed. This solved an age-old problem: how to figure out the path of a cannonball.

ON A ROLL

In addition to rolling balls down ramps, Galileo rolled them over level surfaces and flung them around his room. He measured their tracks with enormous care and timed their every movement, using his pulse as a stopwatch (since clocks hadn't yet been invented). And he made an amazing discovery. The falling balls went faster and faster, with the pull of gravity speeding them up continually, but a ball rolling along a flat surface kept a constant speed *without any force*. Galileo had discovered **inertia**: the tendency of an object either to keep going or to stay still unless a force is acting on it.

I've seen things you people wouldn't believe ...

GALILEO THE ASTRONOMER

Galileo was brilliant at everything he did. In 1609 he heard about the invention of the telescope and set about making his own. It was the best in the world. Using it, he discovered mountains on the Moon, moons around Jupiter, and fantastic numbers of tiny stars, which hinted at the vast size of the universe. What he saw convinced him Copernicus was right about Earth going around the Sun, and he said so in a book in 1632. But religious leaders weren't impressed. They banned the book and imprisoned Galileo.

1609   1632

Galileo
(1564-1642)

GALILEO'S FISH

Galileo's discovery of inertia led him to realize that there's actually no difference between moving at a steady speed and being still. He put it like this in a book: imagine a fish swimming in a tank on a ship that's sailing on the sea. As far as the fish is concerned, the ship might as well be still. The fish doesn't get pushed to the back of the tank by the ship's motion—it swims normally. For just the same reason, clouds and birds don't get left behind and buildings don't fall over as Earth spins around—they all keep moving around with everything else, because they have inertia. Galileo had solved the most puzzling problem with the theory that Earth goes around the Sun.

Newton's
universe

Galileo died in 1642, a prisoner in his home. Fortunately, on Christmas Day of the same year, an even **brighter** scientist was born in England. He was bad tempered, miserable, and peculiar, but he was also a **genius**. His name was **Isaac Newton**.

In 1666 Newton went to stay on his mother's farm to avoid the deadly plague that was sweeping through English towns. One day in the orchard, he saw an apple falling from a tree. He began to wonder if **gravity**, the force that pulled the apple to the ground, might also hold the Moon in its grip.

1666 *and beyond ...*

Hmm... *I can sense* **GRAVITY** *in action!*

Before Newton, nobody understood what kept the Moon flying around Earth, or the planets flying around the Sun. People had always thought they were moved by the gods or pushed along by some invisible force, but Newton **figured out the true answer**.

Isaac Newton
(1642–1727)

Galileo had already figured out exactly why cannonballs fly along curved paths. Newton realized that the Moon is like a gigantic cannonball that is flying too fast to fall back to the ground. To explain this theory, he drew a diagram showing what would happen if you fired a cannonball faster and faster into space from the top of a mountain. At first it would fall back quickly. As it got faster, its curve would get gentler. Eventually it would fly so fast that its path would be less curved than Earth itself. It would continue flying, forever falling and never landing. In other words, it would be trapped **in orbit**.

Newton realized there was no need for a force to push the Moon along. As Galileo had already discovered, a moving object keeps going because it has **inertia**. Newton saw that inertia keeps objects moving in a straight line unless a force pushes them away. The Moon "wants" to fly in a straight line, but the force of Earth's gravity keeps tugging it back, making it fly in a curve.

Newton's drawing

Newton also realized that planets are "falling" around the Sun in just the same way, trapped in orbit by the Sun's immense gravity. He worked out the precise shapes and speeds of their orbits with math, a fantastically complicated task that took years to complete, and forced him to invent a whole new branch of math called calculus. But it was worth it. He'd succeeded in figuring out both gravity and three "laws of motion" that govern how *everything in the universe* moves, from atoms to galaxies. It was the greatest scientific discovery ever.

A 19th-century model of the planets of the solar system, with the Sun in the middle

Nasty Newton

Isaac Newton hated people and spent most of his life alone. At school he was a strange boy with few friends and spent his free time making strange contraptions, such as a kind of windmill powered by mice. As an adult he was always quarreling. He accused other scientists of stealing his ideas, and he once told his mother and stepfather that he was going to burn down their house and kill them. Even his scientific work was sometimes odd, at least by today's standards. He wasted years trying to find a recipe for gold (which is impossible), and he used the Bible to calculate the year of creation as 3500 BC—off by 4.5 billion years.

by the same *force* that makes an apple fall

Physics started with the
idea of forces. So what exactly is a force
and how does it work? Is it something you
can capture in a bottle or examine under
a microscope? Does it glow in the dark or
fizz if you drop it in water? Well... no.

A force isn't really a physical
thing—it's more of an idea.

And a pretty simple idea at that,
because a force is just a *push or a pull*.
Understanding forces can answer all kinds
of questions, like why roller coasters push
your stomach up into your chest, why cats
can jump off skyscrapers and live to tell the
tale, and why a bicycle can accelerate
faster than a sports car.

What is a FORCE?

Forget Star Wars—a force is not some mysterious, invisible energy field that pervades the whole universe. (Though mysterious, invisible energy fields that pervade the whole universe do exist.) It's actually something very simple: just a push or a pull.

In a game of tug-of-war, each team tries to yank the opposing team forward by exerting a more powerful force on the rope. But if the forces balance, nobody moves.

These sumo wrestlers are both leaning forward as they try to push their opponent away with their body weight. Since they weigh the same amount, the forces balance and neither wrestler moves.

PUSH

Some forces can *push and pull* objects without even touching them.

There are forces acting on you *all the time*, whether you know it or not. While you read this, gravity is pulling you down, the ground is pushing you up, air is squeezing you from every direction, and the matter in your body is pushing back at the air. When forces balance, they cancel out and you don't notice them. But when forces *don't* balance, things happen...

Gravity is trying to pull this house back to the ground, but its enormous weight is balanced by an upward supporting force from the ground, transmitted through the truck.

As the boxer's fist delivers a powerful force to the punching bag, it tries to swing back under the force of its own weight. But the forces don't balance, so the punching bag swings to the right.

PULL

It's *the* LAW!

While he was figuring out how gravity governs the movements of the planets, **Isaac Newton** discovered three simple laws that describe how forces make things move. These "laws of motion" laid the foundation for the whole science of physics, and they work for just about everything, from fleas to footballs and from atoms to planets.

1 An object that isn't being pushed or pulled by a force either *stays still* or *keeps moving* in a straight line at a constant speed.

2 *Forces* make things accelerate. The bigger the force, and the lighter the object, the *greater the acceleration*.

3 Every action has an *equal* and *opposite* reaction.

... in other words

if you let go of a moving shopping cart,
it keeps going in a straight line until it
crashes into something.
This law is all about *inertia*. It's common sense
that an object stays still until something pushes it, but
what about the second half of the law? In our everyday
experience, moving objects don't keep on going forever
at a constant speed—they grind to a halt. That's because
friction and other forces are slowing them down. But
if you take away friction—by wearing ice skates,
sitting in a shopping cart, or going into space—
Newton's first law works much better.

... in other words

it's much easier to make a lightweight
racing bike speed up than a ten-ton truck.
This law tells you exactly what happens when you give
something a push. In everyday language, "acceleration"
means speeding up, and that's what happens if you push
something forward. The harder you push the pedals on
a bike, the faster you go. And the less you and your
bike weigh, the easier it is to speed up. In physics,
acceleration doesn't just mean speeding up—it can
mean *any change* from either being still or
traveling in a straight line at a steady speed.
So when you pull on your brakes to slow down,
the force of friction gives you *negative*
acceleration (you decelerate).

... in other words

when a rocket pushes burning gas out of its engine,
the gas pushes back on the rocket and lifts it into space.
Newton realized that forces (which he called "actions")
always happen in pairs. If one object pushes
another, the second object pushes back with the same
force. The forces are equal, but their effects may not be.
If you throw a ball, the ball pushes back on your hand,
but only the ball flies away. If you push the ground
quickly with your feet, the ground pushes back and flings
you into the air—you jump. The force from your feet
also moves the whole of planet Earth down, but only by
a tiny amount!

Can you *do* PHYSICS

To see how Newton's laws
work, all you have to do is get
on a bike and go for a ride...

(1)

Setting off
Before you set off, your
bike is standing still
because there's no force
acting on it. That's
Newton's first law at
work. When you get on
and start pedaling, you
apply a force and the
bike accelerates. That's
Newton's second law. If
the bike is very light,
you'll accelerate quickly.
That's also Newton's
second law.

2

Downhill
You start going down
a hill. Now another force
is making you accelerate:
gravity. You go faster and
faster without having to
pedal. In fact, you're
going a bit too fast so
you apply the brakes
sharply. They rub the
wheels, using the
force of friction
to slow you
down.

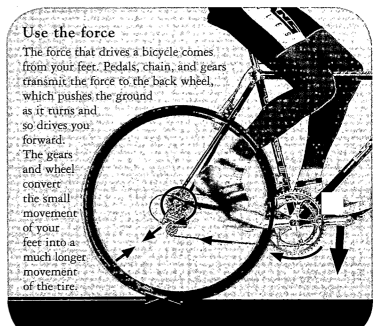

Use the force
The force that drives a bicycle comes
from your feet. Pedals, chain, and gears
transmit the force to the back wheel,
which pushes the ground
as it turns and
so drives you
forward.
The gears
and wheel
convert
the small
movement
of your
feet into a
much longer
movement
of the tire.

③

④

Wipeout
Yikes! You must have
pulled on the brakes too
hard. The bike stopped,
but you didn't. Inertia
kept your body moving
in a straight line at a
constant speed and you
flew over the handlebars.
Blame Newton's first law.
You get back on the bike
and coast downhill again.

Freewheeling
When you reach the
bottom of the hill you
stop accelerating, but you
don't have to pedal just
yet—you can freewheel.
Your bike keeps moving
at a steady speed because
of Newton's first law.
Now your body's inertia
is helping you.

What a drag
The main thing holding you back as you cycle along the flat is
"drag"—a complicated kind of friction caused by air. Low posture,
smooth clothes, and a streamlined helmet can all help to reduce it.

... on a *bike?*

On the flat

As you freewheel along the flat, you lose speed. But Newton's first law says moving objects keep going at a steady speed, unless there's a force. So there must be a force. It's friction again, but this time it's caused mostly by the air pushing against you. To maintain your speed, you have to pedal just enough to balance the force of friction.

Uphill

Now gravity is pulling the bike again, but this time it's working against you. Thanks to Newton's second law, gravity makes you decelerate. Gravity is more powerful than friction with the air, so you have to pedal much harder to overcome it. Cycling uphill is hard!

Turning

The road bends, so you steer the handlebars to make a turn. Newton's first law says you should keep going straight unless there's a force, so where's the force? It's actually friction again. When you turn, friction between your wheels and road becomes one-sided, pushing you away from a straight line.

7

5

6

> *You* **WILL** *obey my laws!*
> *... and I recommend a cycle helmet—you never know when you might need to protect your head!*

Get a grip

So where does Newton's *third law* come in? The third law explains why a bike works at all. As you force the back wheel around, its tire grips the ground and pushes it. The ground pushes back equally, driving you forward.

8

What *causes* FRICTION?

No matter how smooth an object might look, in reality it's covered with millions of tiny jagged bumps and dents. When two objects rub together, the tiny bumps snag each other and slow the objects down. This slowing force is *friction*, and it's the enemy of motion. But sometimes it's a good thing, because friction also gives you grip.

HOW TO BEAT FRICTION

One way to beat friction is to cover moving objects with a slippery liquid—a lubricant. If all the moving parts on a bicycle are well lubricated with oil, the bicycle will be more efficient because less energy is wasted in friction. Even solids can act as lubricants. Snow and sand are both slippery enough to ski down because they are made of small grains that slide past each other.

NOW TRY THIS!

To prove how powerful friction can be, interleave the pages of two paperback books. Challenge a friend to pull them apart with strength alone. They won't be able to!

How do flies walk up walls?

Flies can run up walls and scamper over ceilings, so why don't they fall off? Friction is part of the answer, and their feet also have tiny hooks for hanging onto crevices. But the real secret of their sticky feet is soft pads covered with hundreds of tiny, damp hairs. The hairs mold to the shape of any surface and form a sticky seal.

FACT OR FRICTION

TRACTION CONTROL

Walking would be impossible without friction. If there were no friction between your feet and the ground, your shoes wouldn't grip and you'd slip with every step. Shoes and tires with a deeply patterned tread give maximum grip, or "traction," ideal for slippery surfaces.

TWO TYPES OF FRICTION

There are two types of friction: static friction and sliding friction. Static friction is much more powerful and makes it hard to budge an object that isn't moving, like a heavy box on the floor. Once the box *is* moving, you can push it fairly easily, because only the weaker force of sliding friction is trying to slow it down.

It won't budge!

STATIC FRICTION

Easy!

SLIDING FRICTION

What happens when you skid?

Cars and bikes normally grip the road with **static friction**. When a wheel goes into a skid, however, the point of contact slides over the ground, so the only force gripping the surface is **sliding friction**. Because sliding friction is weaker than static friction, cars and bikes have much less grip when they skid and are harder to control.

Balls of steel

Bearings do the same job as lubricants, reducing friction between moving parts. Bicycles have bearings in the wheels, pedals, and the tube under the handlebars.

SLIP

FACT OR FRICTION

Antilock braking

Used properly, bike brakes should always create sliding friction. If you brake too hard, static friction takes over and the wheel locks, causing a skid. On icy roads the tires have much less grip and can skid very easily. If you ride on ice, brake little and often and use the back brake only.

Making fire

Whenever friction happens, some of the movement energy in an object turns into heat energy. (Rub your hands together as hard as you can for proof.) If there's enough friction, the heat can trigger a fire. People first realized this about half a million years ago when someone had the brilliant idea of rubbing two sticks together.

Get a grip

Ever wondered what your fingerprints are actually *for?* The answer is friction. They work the same way as the soles of shoes or the tread of a tire. The ridges of skin also have tiny pores that ooze water and oil to make them stickier.

velocity = distance ÷ time

How *FAST*

On Earth, moving objects don't usually keep going in a straight line at a constant speed—they're always speeding up,

To figure out your speed, divide how far you travel by how long it takes. So if you run 24 miles (or kilometers) in 2 hours, your speed is 12 mph (or km/h). Physicists usually talk about *velocity* rather than speed. Velocity is your speed in a particular direction. If you run north and turn east without slowing, your velocity north drops to zero but your speed doesn't change.

How fast can you go on Earth?

How fast you can go depends on where you are. Traveling in water is slow because water creates lots of friction. In fact, the world's fastest submarine is slower than a bus. On land, friction with the ground can hold you back. Only one land vehicle has exceeded the 760 mph (1,224 km/h) speed of sound—a British car called *Thrust SSC*. Traveling faster than sound is easier in air, where jets routinely break the sound barrier, causing weird cloud formations and sonic booms.

How fast can you go in space?

In space, where there's no air to cause friction, spacecraft can reach thousands of miles per hour. But it feels just the same as being still. You only feel the effect of motion in space if you *accelerate*. And no matter how powerful your rocket, you can't exceed 670 million mph (1 billion km/h)—the speed of light. It's the ultimate speed limit.

How fast is the fastest... space probe?

... manned spacecraft?

... car?

... production car?

... cyclist?

... caravan tow?

... land animal?   62 mph (100 km/h) cheetah

... tank?

... submarine?   46 mph (74 km/h) *Russian Alpha*

... insect? 36

... person?   27 mph (43 km/h)

can *you GO*?

slowing down, and changing direction. To understand what they're doing, you need to know their *velocity* and *acceleration*.

acceleration = change in velocity ÷ time

Acceleration is how quickly your velocity is changing. It's a tricky concept to understand. It doesn't just mean speeding up—it means *any change in velocity*. Speeding up and slowing down both count as acceleration, and so does changing direction, because velocity has a direction.

What's the force you feel?

Unlike speed, acceleration is something you really *feel*. When a powerful car accelerates, you feel pushed into the back of the seat by invisible hands. Likewise, you feel pushed forward when you decelerate, and you feel pushed sideways when you turn. This pushing feeling isn't a real force—it's just your inertia trying to keep you moving in a straight line at a steady speed. But it feels just like the force of gravity, so we call it *g* force. When you ride in a lift, *g* force acts in the same direction as real gravity, making you feel heavier or lighter than you really are.

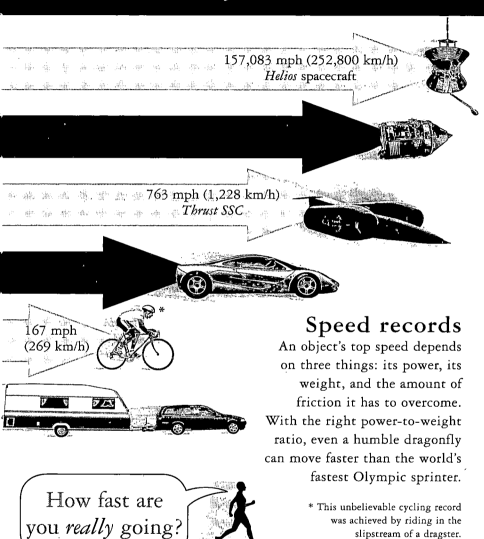

157,083 mph (252,800 km/h)
Helios spacecraft

763 mph (1,228 km/h)
Thrust SSC

167 mph
(269 km/h) *

Speed records

An object's top speed depends on three things: its power, its weight, and the amount of friction it has to overcome. With the right power-to-weight ratio, even a humble dragonfly can move faster than the world's fastest Olympic sprinter.

* This unbelievable cycling record was achieved by riding in the slipstream of a dragster.

How fast are you *really* going?

Speed is relative. You probably think you're sitting quite still as you read this, but think for a moment: Planet Earth is spinning around, which means you're actually traveling east at up to 1,000 mph (1,600 km/h). And Earth isn't just spinning—it's flying around the Sun at more than 70,000 mph (110,000 km/h) (which means you are too). Then again, the Sun and the solar system are hurtling through space at 1.3 million mph (2 million km/h). So how fast are you *really* going? There's no right answer—it just depends on your point of view.

GOING UP	GOING DOWN
g force makes you feel heavier	*g* force makes you feel lighter

G FORCE

The *exhilarating feelings* you get on a roller coaster are caused by g force. With every twist, turn, rise, and fall, the train is changing speed. And every time it changes speed or direction, g force pushes your body.

G force acts on every part of your body, including your internal organs, which are only loosely connected together. As you plunge downhill, your stomach and intestines lurch upward and press against the base of your lungs. And as the train turns up at the bottom of a valley, all your internal organs are squished downward.

At the bottom of a hill on a big roller coaster, g force *triples* your body weight.

At the crest of a roller coaster hill you experience *negative g force*. It acts in the opposite direction to gravity, canceling your weight and making you float upward. The front and back seats get the most powerful negative *g*'s because they ride over the crest quickest.

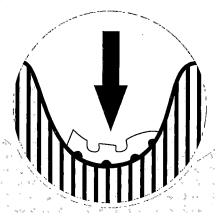

At the bottom of a valley you feel *positive g force*, which multiplies the force of gravity and presses you into your chair, making you up to three times heavier. The middle seat gets the highest positive *g* force because it passes through the bottom of the valley quickest.

A fighter pilot endures up to 9 *g* in sharp turns. This tremendous force pushes blood out of his head and into his legs, which can make him pass out unless he wears a pressure suit and performs forceful clenching movements with lower body muscles during the turn.

In 1954, US scientist John Paul Stapp subjected himself to 46.2 *g* in the name of science. Strapped into a rocket-powered sled on train tracks, he decelerated from 630 mph (1,017 km/h) to zero in 1.25 seconds—equivalent to hitting a brick wall at 120 mph (190 km/h). He survived (there was no brick wall), but his eyes filled with blood and he was temporarily blinded—a "red out."

Can you take the *g*'s?

The human body can barely withstand negative *g* force as it pushes blood up into your head and can burst blood vessels in your brain. However, people have survived brief exposure to amazing high positive *g*'s.

−3 *g*	The maximum negative *g* force a person can safely withstand.
0 *g*	Weightlessness in space.
1 *g*	Normal gravity.
3 *g*	The maximum *g* force experienced on a big roller coaster.
4.3 *g*	The maximum *g* force civilian aircraft are designed to take.
5 *g*	Most people black out if subjected to more than 5 *g* for a sustained period.
5.1 *g*	Top dragsters can do 0 to 60 mph (100 km/h) in half a second, producing 5.1 *g*.
9 *g*	Fighter pilots are trained to withstand 9 *g* during aerial maneuvers.
46.2 *g*	The maximum *g* force deliberately endured by a human being.
100 *g*	Exposure to 100 *g*, however brief, is nearly always fatal.
180 *g*	The maximum *g* force a human being has survived.

TYPES OF ENERGY

 Potential energy is the energy you store when you lift up a weight, squeeze a spring, or stretch an elastic band.

 Chemical energy is trapped in molecules. Food, gas, and other types of fuel are rich in chemical energy.

 Kinetic energy is the energy a moving object has. The faster something is moving, the more kinetic energy it has.

 Light is pure energy traveling at an amazing speed. Nearly all the energy we use comes originally from sunlight.

 Heat is the energy of atoms and molecules shaking. The hotter something gets, the faster the atoms shake.

 Electrical energy is a form of energy that can travel conveniently through wires with almost no waste.

Dark energy is a mysterious form of energy that is making the universe expand.

Nuclear energy is released when atoms are torn apart or fused together in the Sun, nuclear bombs, and nuclear power plants.

ENERGY

Forces can't happen without ENERGY. Whenever a force pushes or pulls something, energy is making it happen. Without energy, nothing in the universe would happen.

Light energy

Maximize your potential

Stored energy is sometimes called potential energy. As you climb the hill at the start of a roller coaster, your potential energy builds up. When you ride downhill, the potential energy turns into kinetic energy, making you go faster and faster.

I've got maximum potential energy!

HOW DOES ENERGY WORK?

Energy works a bit like money. You can save it up or you can spend it and make things happen. The energy you save isn't doing anything while it's in storage, but it does have the *potential* to make things happen. Using it is like spending money. You get something in return—like light from a flashlight—but you end up with less in your store.

FAQ

How do you measure energy?
Scientists measure energy in joules. One joule is about the amount of energy you need to lift an apple up by 3 ft (1 m). A light bulb uses about 100 joules a second, a person sprinting uses about 1,000, and a car uses about 100,000. One slice of cherry pie contains 2,000,000 joules—enough to drive a car for 20 seconds or to lift two million apples by 3 ft (1 m).

Where does energy come from?
Whenever you turn on a light, watch TV, or ride in a car, you're using energy. Most energy we use comes from fossil fuels, which are burned in power plants so the energy can be converted into other forms. Fossil fuels are called nonrenewable energy because they'll run out one day. Other types of energy, such as solar power, are called renewable, because there's an unlimited supply.

$$E = mc^2$$

When an atom bomb explodes, some of the matter turns into pure energy. Albert Einstein's famous equation tells you exactly how much energy (E) you get. To work out the energy in joules, you multiply the amount of matter in kilograms (m) by a *colossal* number: the speed of light squared (c^2). That's why atom bombs make such a big bang!

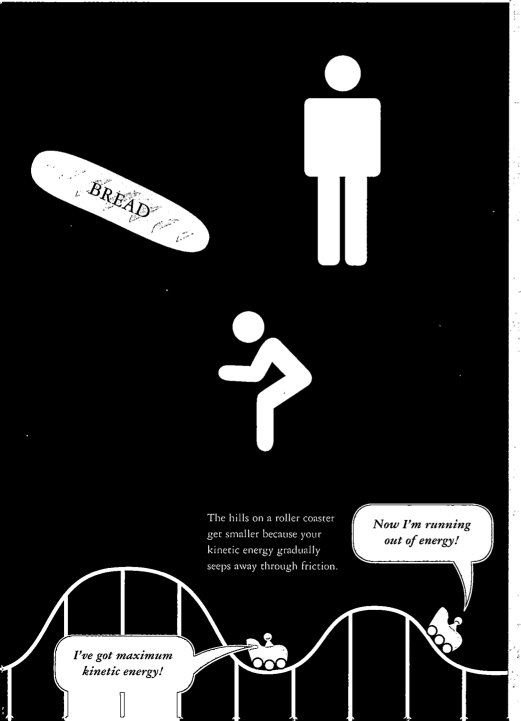

The hills on a roller coaster get smaller because your kinetic energy gradually seeps away through friction.

Now I'm running out of energy!

I've got maximum kinetic energy!

How can you make

Any gadget that magnifies a force is called a MACHINE. Most of the machines you use are so simple you probably don't even realize they're machines. Door handles, hammers, can openers, and wheels all count as machines.

Machines work on a very simple principle: you put in a force at one end and you get a different-size force—usually a bigger one—out the other end. Try pulling a nail out of wood with your fingers. With a claw hammer it's easy, because the hammer *magnifies the force.*

small force, long distance

The INCLINED PLANE

The simplest kind of machine is the inclined plane, which is just a fancy term for a ramp. It's much easier to carry a heavy load up a long ramp than it is to haul it up vertically. But you have to carry it much farther, and that's the catch.

The LEVER

A lever is a machine with a fixed point—a *fulcrum*—that stays still while other parts move. As a result, the lever pivots. Depending on what type of lever it is, the force you put in can be either magnified or shrunk.

Pliers turn the weak force of your hand into a more powerful gripping force on the other side of the fulcrum. The magnified force moves a shorter distance.

fulcrum

The WHEEL

As well as rolling along the ground to help things move, wheels can magnify or reduce forces in a similar way to levers. The bigger the wheel, the more it changes the size of the forces.

A steering wheel turns the weak force from your hands into a powerful force at the hub. The rear wheel of a bike does the opposite, turning a powerful force from the chain into a weak force at the tire, but it multiplies the distance.

FORCES bigger?

Machines don't give you something for nothing. There's a catch: the magnified force moves a *shorter distance* than the force you put in. So what you gain in force, you pay for in distance.

To put it another way, the energy you put in equals the energy you get out, because you have to obey this law:

energy used = force × distance

The WEDGE

A wedge works like a ramp, except that it moves. An ax is a wedge. When an ax hits a log, the long downward force is transmitted into much more powerful (but shorter) sideways forces that split the wood.

The SCREW

A screw is simply an inclined plane that's been coiled up. Each turn of a screw pushes it just a tiny bit deeper into the wood, but with much greater force than your hand applies at the other end. A big screwdriver makes the job even easier.

large force, short distance

fulcrum

Nutcrackers turn the weak force of your hand into a powerful crunching force on the same side of the fulcrum, but nearer to it.

fulcrum

Chopsticks reduce the force of your fingers but magnify their movements, giving a more delicate grip.

GEARS

A gear is a wheel with teeth that turns a second, similar wheel. In a car engine the gears make direct contact, but in a bicycle they are linked by a chain. If the first wheel has more teeth than the second, the second one turns faster but with less force. If the second wheel has more teeth than the first wheel, it turns slower but with more force.

lift *a truck with* one hand

How do bicycles work?

The bicycle is the *most efficient transportation machine* invented, turning the energy you supply into pure forward motion. So how does it work?

To stay balanced a cyclist has to keep adjusting the front wheel, which therefore makes a wavier track than the rear wheel.

Front track

Rear track

To steer you just turn the handlebars the way you want to go, don't you? Wrong. Cyclists actually steer with their body weight and use the handlebars mainly for balance. In fact, to turn left you *steer right* a little first, which tips your weight to the left. This is called countersteering and it happens without thinking. Don't do it deliberately—you'll probably fall off!

REAR SPOKES cross each other rather than radiating straight from the hub. Being slightly off-center helps them bear the twisting force that turns the wheel.

GEARS control the speed and force of the rear wheel. A high gear converts one turn of your feet into several turns of the rear wheel—ideal for speeding along flat surfaces. Low gears turn the rear wheel slower but with more force—ideal for cycling uphill.

WHEELS do two jobs. First, the rear wheel transmits the pushing force from your legs to the ground, driving the bicycle forward. Second, both wheels reduce friction by rolling over a small point of contact. The thinner the wheel and the tighter the tire, the less the friction and the faster you go.

If you pull the front brake suddenly, your inertia can send you hurtling over the handlebars. The secret to safe stopping is to brake gradually and to keep the front and back brakes balanced. In wet weather, brake slower and longer.

TIRES provide just enough friction to grip the ground. The air inside makes them elastic, helping absorb shocks.

PEDALS convert the up-and-down motion of your legs into rotation. They also work as levers, magnifying the force from the legs to pull the chain.

HOW WAS THE BICYCLE INVENTED?

1817

The world's first bicycle was the "dandy horse"—a wooden running machine used as a substitute for a horse. You ran on the ground and pushed the ground with your feet, steering the front wheel by hand.

1863

Pedals were added to the front, which in 1870s resulted in the "velocipede." You would ride slim, without gears, but your feet provided force only if you wanted to go fast.

1872

For more speed, people made the front wheel bigger. The "high-wheeler" was fast but dangerously unstable. It was all too easy to fall off, and falls were reputed to land head-first. Ouch!

AIR FLOW

HANDLEBARS

are levers that make it easy to turn the front wheel. The wider the handlebars, the easier it is to make fine adjustments to the wheel. Racing bikes have "drop handlebars" to help you keep your head down, which reduces drag.

BRAKES grip the wheel

rims to create friction and slow you down. The bike's energy doesn't just disappear though—it turns into sound (hence the squealing) and heat. Try touching the wheel rims after slamming on the brakes to see how hot they get.

A clever way to reduce drag is to cycle just behind another cyclist, where invisible whirlpools in the air give you an extra push. This is called "drafting" and it can cut your energy use by up to 40 percent.

Using energy

A bicycle turns 90 percent of the energy you supply into movement energy, making it the most efficient transportation machine in the world. A car converts only 25 percent of its energy into movement energy, and most of that is used shifting its own huge weight. In fact, the energy you use to cycle 0.6 miles (1 km) would shift a car only 66 ft (20 m). You need less energy to cycle 0.6 miles (1 km) than to travel by car, train, horse, or even to run or walk.

Cycling

Walking

Running

Scooter

Train with passengers

Car with 5 passengers

Horse riding

Swimming

Car with 1 passenger

| 0 | 200 | 400 | 600 | 800 | 1000 |

Energy needed to transport
a person 0.6 mile (1 km) in kcal

1884

1893

2006

How *fast* can you FALL?

What's your limit?

Your terminal velocity depends on your shape and weight. Something very light and fluffy, like a dandelion seed, catches so much air that is has almost zero terminal velocity and can float. The terminal velocity of rain is 17 mph (27 km/h), which is about as fast as a person running. The terminal velocity of a cat is 62 mph (100 km/h), which is half that of a human being and just low enough for a cat to survive a fall from the top of a skyscraper.

Can you fall faster?

Skydivers vary their terminal velocity by changing their posture. Normally a skydiver splays his arms and legs to create as much drag as possible and to stop himself from tumbling randomly. In this position, called a "stable spread," his terminal velocity is about 125 mph (200 km/h) and he can open a parachute safely. To speed up, he either "stands up" or dives headfirst with his arms and legs held straight behind him. In this more streamlined posture he can reach 180 mph (290 km/h).

A good way to find out how the force of **GRAVITY** works is to jump out of a plane. Gravity pulls your body every moment of your life, but there's usually something solid under you to counteract its effect. So what happens when there's nothing to break your fall?

Forces make things *accelerate*. The moment you step out of plane, gravity pulls you down with as much acceleration as a McLaren F1, the world's fastest production sports car. In only 3 seconds you pass 62 mph (100 km/h). But you don't accelerate all the way down. As you speed up, friction with the air (drag) gets stronger and stronger, until the wind roaring past feels like a hurricane. Ten seconds into the the jump, the force of drag balances the pull of gravity and you stop accelerating. You've reached **TERMINAL VELOCITY**.

DRAG

Although gravity seems like impressive stuff when you're plunging to Earth at 124 mph (200 km/h), it's actually the **weakest force in the universe**. All objects pull on each other with gravity, but so weakly that we never notice. It takes an entire planetful of matter to create a noticeable amount of gravity.

FAQ

How do parachutes work?

Parachutes work by increasing the drag. When a parachute first opens, the sudden increase in drag makes the skydiver decelerate violently until his velocity drops to about 12 mph (20 km/h). If there were no air, a skydiver would accelerate all the way down, even with his chute open, and would hit the ground at more than 620 mph (1,000 km/h).

What's the highest skydive?

The world's highest skydive took place in August 1960 when US pilot Joseph Kittinger leapt from a helium balloon at 102,800 ft (31,330 m) altitude—3.5 times higher than the summit of Mount Everest. Air is thinner at great heights and causes much less drag. Kittinger reached a terminal velocity of 614 mph (989 km/h)—faster than a speeding bullet—and so became the fastest unaided human being in history.

GRAVITY

Blowing in *the wind*

This is what the force of drag can do to a human face without the protection of a mask or visor. As the wind speed increases from 275 mph (440 km/h) to 350 mph (560 km/h), the blasting air stretches your skin and rips your mouth open. Skydivers never experience this much drag, but fighter pilots can do if they eject from jet aircraft in an emergency.

How do PLANES

What's the best shape for flight?

The ideal shape for a plane depends on what job it has to do. Long wings make planes more efficient but slower and harder to turn. Short wings are better for maneuverability.

Fighter jets like the Eurofighter Typhoon have short, stubby wings that allow them to make very sharp turns in the air.

The bigger the cargo hold, the more a plane can carry. The Boeing Super Guppy can swallow and carry whole planes up to 29 tons (26 metric tons).

Since their wings rotate, helicopters don't have to move forward to create lift. As a result, they can hover and fly backward or sideways.

Flapping wings make insects more agile than aircraft. Bees flap their wings 200 times a second but some midges flap 1,000 times a second.

If you flatten your hand, angle it up a little, and very carefully hold it outside the window of a moving car, you'll feel a force pushing it upward. The force is *LIFT* and it keeps planes in the air. So where does the force of lift come from?

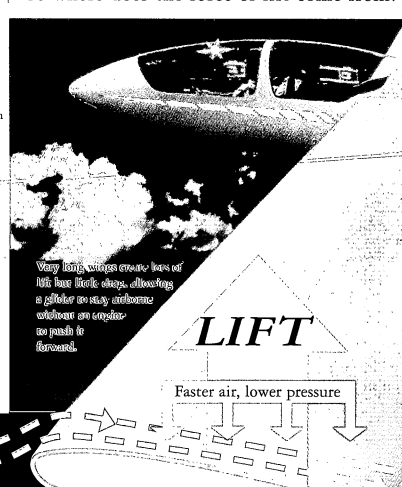

Very long wings create lots of lift but little drag, allowing a glider to stay airborne without an engine to push it forward.

LIFT

Faster air, lower pressure

airflow

Slower air, higher pressure

THE WING of a plane isn't just angled upward like your hand was—it also has a special shape called an aerofoil, which is rounded on top but flatter on the bottom. Both the angle and the shape cause air to flow faster over the top of the wing than beneath it. Fast-moving air has lower pressure than slow air,

stay in the AIR?

Newton's third law tells you where lift comes from. When you hold your hand out of the car window, it pushes the flowing air down. So the air must be pushing back up with an equal and opposite force. Your hand is also pushing forward, and that's matched by an equal and opposite force pushing it back—*DRAG*.

Levitating ball trick

Planes rely on the fact that slow-moving air has a higher pressure than fast-moving air. This is called the Bernoulli effect, and you can see it for yourself by performing a magic trick. Place a ping-pong ball in the flow of air above a hairdryer and the ball will get trapped. When it tries to fall out, the slow-moving air outside the main flow pushes it back because it has greater pressure.

high pressure · high pressure

A jumbo jet pushes a huge "river" of air down behind it, generating enormous lift.

The behind a can flip a small plane UPSIDE DOWN

What a waste

At the tip of a plane's wing, high-pressure air from below the wing swirls up to the low-pressure area on top. The swirling movement creates a whirlpool in the air—a vortex. The vortex

Why do GOLF BALLS have dimples?

While planes usually need to be as smooth and streamlined as possible to fly, the opposite is true of golf balls. The 300 or so dimples on a golf ball make it fly up to three times farther than a smooth ball would. Here's how...

Flowing air

Wide zone of turbulent air

Flight path

The drag that slows down a flying ball is caused partly by friction and partly by something called *turbulence*. Turbulent air is full of whirlpools that steal kinetic energy from the ball, slowing it down. A smooth ball creates a wide zone of turbulence behind it and so loses a lot of its energy.

Flowing air breaks away.

Flowing air hugs the ball's surface.

Dimples roughen the layer of air flowing immediately over a golf ball. For reasons nobody quite understands, this makes the flowing air stick to the surface for longer before breaking away. As a result, the zone of turbulent air is narrower and causes much less drag.

Narrow zone of turbulent air

Flight path

Only balls with evenly spaced dimples are allowed in golf. Uneven patterns are banned because they can make the ball fly too well!

HOW DO BULLETS WORK?

This incredible high-speed photo reveals what happens to the air as a bullet leaves the barrel of a gun. Moving at supersonic speed (faster than sound), the bullet leaves a V-shaped trail and a spherical shockwave of sound—the BANG—filled with a cloud of exploded gunpowder.

Can you *bend it like* BECKHAM?

A professional soccer player can not only make a soccer ball curve, but can also kick it so it seems to be going straight but turns at the last instant and slips inside the goalpost. The secret to this trick is the MAGNUS EFFECT.

5. Because the air pressure is higher on the right side, the ball is pushed to the left and bends as it flies.

GOAL!

3. On this side the whirlpool of air moves *against* the oncoming air, which increases the air pressure.

4. On this side the whirlpool moves the *same way* as the oncoming air, which reduces the pressure.

2. The spinning ball drags the layer of air on its surface around with it, forming a whirlpool of air.

The Magnus effect works best at certain speeds. A very fast ball hardly curves at all, but a slow ball curves strongly. A skilled player can control when the curve will happen by giving the ball just the right combination of speed and spin. As a result, he can make a ball fly almost straight and curve into the net at the last moment, as it loses speed.

1. The player strikes the ball off center to make it spin.

groove cut into it. The groove makes the bullet spin as it flies, creating a special kind of inertia (gyroscopic inertia) that stops the bullet from tilting. A spinning bullet follows a very straight

phenomenal kinetic energy, due to their speed, which can easily exceed 600 mph (1,000 km/h). It's this energy that makes

Why don't cars take off?

For fast cars, staying on the ground can be a challenge. Air tries to flow under as well as over a car, which can make the whole vehicle act like a wing and try to lift off as speed rises. A 400-ton (360-metric ton) jumbo jet only has to reach 180 mph (290 km/h) to take off, so how does a 1-ton Ferrari stay down at 186 mph (300 km/h)? One solution is to add a spoiler—an upside-down wing on the rear of a car. A spoiler creates negative lift, pushing the rear wheels down and improving grip.

Speed machine

As with planes, cars are shaped to suit the job they do. Dragsters are built purely for acceleration in a straight line. A very long body and spoilers at both the front and rear counter the dragster's tendency to lift off the road. Massive rear wheels deliver the pushing force, accelerating the car from 0 to 330 mph (530 km/h) in under 5 seconds.

What's the best *shape*

The shape of cars has changed a lot in the last 100 years. The first cars looked like giant baby buggies, sounded like tractors, and were barely faster than walking speed.

Mild turbulence

Severe turbulence

KEEP A LOW PROFILE

Aerodynamics is the study of the way air flows around objects. A car has to push a hole through the air as it moves, which gets increasingly difficult as speed increases. So the first rule of aerodynamics is to keep the hole small. Instead of making a car tall and square, make it long and flat.

Dragster

Wind tunnels

In the past, designers built clay or metal models of cars and tested their aerodynamics in a wind tunnel (left), which blows a jet of air and smoke over the car to reveal the shape of the airflow. These days the job can be done by computers that model the physics of flowing air (right), allowing a car's shape to be perfected without the expense of a real model.

for a CAR?

Today's supercars are altogether sleeker, flatter, curvier, and, of course, faster. So why do they look so different? In a word: **AERODYNAMICS.**

DON'T STIR THINGS UP

The next rule is to help the air flow as smoothly as possible. Like golf balls and planes, cars leave a trail of swirling, *turbulent* air behind them, which wastes energy. Boxy shapes with sharp corners create lots of turbulence; smooth, tapering shapes create less.

Keep the weight down

The lighter a car is, the faster it accelerates. The Ariel Atom is a third the weight of an average car and can reach 60 mph (100 km/h) in 2.9 seconds. To keep the weight down it has no roof or body (but there is plenty of room for an umbrella).

Lie flat

Solar-powered cars are as flat as pancakes to minimize drag, but the driver has to lie down. The flat shape also provides room for the car's solar panels.

Channel the airflow

By taking in air at the front and channeling it at high speed under its bodywork, the Pagani Zonda creates a low pressure zone below that helps keep its lightweight carbon body pressed down.

What not to drive

Before car designers started using wind tunnels, they made cars *look* streamlined but got the physics wrong. The Lamborghini Miura of the 1960s was the top supercar of its day. It was sleek, sophisticated, and fast—but totally unsteerable above 150 mph (240 km/h) because the wheels wouldn't stay on the road.

A Formula One car gets a workout in a computer-generated airflow test. The program can isolate different parts of the airflow, such as the air moving through the engine bay and around the wheels as they spin.

Why do balls b^ounce?

If you drop a beanbag on the ground, it loses all its kinetic energy and sits there in a heap. But a bouncy ball squeezes like a spring and stores its energy as *potential energy*. As it rebounds, the stored energy turns back into kinetic energy and pushes the ball up again.

warm balls bounce highest

A tennis ball loses nearly half its kinetic energy each time it hits the ground, so each bounce is only about half as high as the last one.

Newton's cradle

Objects that conserve kinetic energy when they hit something are called *elastic*. Steel balls are so elastic they can pass their energy along a row with very little loss. In a "Newton's cradle," when one ball is swung to hit the others, its energy passes along the line and the last ball springs outward as if by magic.

Try the two-ball bounce

Take two bouncy balls of different sizes and put one on top of the other. Drop them on a hard surface and watch what happens. The bottom ball hits the ground first and then transfers its kinetic energy to the top ball, making it bounce much higher than it would on its own.

When a ball bounces off the ground,
*planet **Earth*** bounces the opposite way a tiny bit

BOUNCE-ability

Balls bounce best when they store energy by
compressing rather than bending. Something bendable,
like a beanbag, won't bounce at all. Solid balls bounce
well (even marbles), and air-filled balls bounce well
only when correctly inflated. The bounciest ball of
all is a steel ball, like the one in Newton's cradle.
It can bounce to 98% of its original height
if you drop it on solid steel.

98%

81%

67%

56%

56%

40%

30%

0%

BEANBAG

BASEBALL

SOCCER BALL

TENNIS BALL

BASKETBALL

GOLF BALL

SUPERBALL

STEEL BALL

INELASTIC

Why don't dogs bounce?

Objects that don't conserve kinetic energy
when they hit something are called
inelastic. Dogs and people are inelastic
because they don't immediately
spring back into their former
shape on hitting something.
But they will bounce if they
hit a very elastic surface,
such as a trampoline.

Inelastic collisions

When two inelastic objects hit each other at high
speed, the kinetic energy goes into changing their
shapes rather than making them bounce apart.
In a car crash this is
actually a good
thing. By crumpling
up, the cars absorb
most of the energy
and so protect the people inside.

Can you *lie* on a bed of nails?

A bed of nails is made of thousands of nails pointing upward. Surely you'd get STABBED thousands of times if you tried to lie down on one? Actually you wouldn't, provided you got on the bed carefully. To find out why not, you have to understand about PRESSURE.

Under pressure

The amount a pushing force is concentrated or spread out is called *pressure*. When you push a thumb tack into a wall, the force from your finger is concentrated into a far smaller area at the other end. As a result, the tack goes into the wall and not your finger. The sharper the point of the tack, the greater the pressure, because:

pressure = force ÷ area

WEAK PRESSURE

STRONG PRESSURE

OUCH!

1

110 lb

Now think about how pressure works with a bed of nails. Let's suppose you weigh 110 lb (50 kg) and you lie on a "bed of one nail." The force of all your weight would be concentrated on one nail. It would hurt—a lot.

NOW TRY THIS

Shrink-wrap your arm

To witness the awesome power of air pressure, remove the sleeve from one of your arms and place your arm in a trash can liner. Use the suction tube of a vacuum cleaner to suck out the air. The pressure of the air outside will press the plastic tight

Make a bed of nails

You can see how a bed of nails works with a packet of thumb tacks and a tomato or a toy animal. (Don't use a real animal.) Start with one tack and see what happens when you let the tomato's weight rest on it. Increase the number of tacks to reduce the pressure until the tomato's weight

WATER PRESSURE

Even liquids and gases put pressure on things. When you swim under water, water molecules press against your body. As you go deeper, the weight of the water above you makes the pressure rise. At just over a half mile (1 km) depth, the force on your skin is about 7 tons per square inch (1 metric ton per square centimeter). Deep-sea divers need special diving suits to withstand such fantastic pressures.

To see how water pressure rises with depth, cut the top off a plastic bottle, make a series of holes down the side, and fill it with water. The bottom jet squirts farthest because pressure is highest.

If you lie on a "bed of ten nails," the pressure on each nail would be a tenth as much, but still a lot. It would be about the same as putting a watermelon on each nail.

AIR PRESSURE

As you read this, the air around you is pushing on your body with a force of about 15 tonnes. If the atoms in your body weren't pushing back equally, you'd be crushed in an instant. When the pressure of air goes up and the volume stays the same, the temperature automatically rises. As you pump up a bike wheel, you can feel the heat of the pressurized air coming through the pump.

Secret squirter

Here's a practical joke to play on nosy snoops. Write "DO NOT OPEN" with a magic marker on a plastic bottle and make holes in the letters with a pin. Fill with water and screw on the lid. The holes won't leak because air pressure keeps the water in. But if a snoop secretly opens the bottle, air gets in the top and they get soaked!

And for my next trick...

Fill a glass tumbler to the brim with water and slide a postcard over the top. Keeping your hand pressed on the card, turn the tumbler upside down over the sink. Take your hand away and the card *should* stay in place, held in place by air pressure!

⊛ What's the MATTER?

Imagine you chopped an apple in half, chopped the halves in half again, and then continued to do this millions of millions of times. Let's assume you had a pretty small knife.

After a few billion years of chopping you'd get to a point where you can't chop any further. You'd have reached the building block that makes up everything in the universe: THE MIGHTY ATOM.

For years, scientists thought atoms were the smallest things possible.

Then someone found you can chop even further, and a strange new world opened up...

What is MATTER

EVERYTHING is made of atoms. Houses, trees, cars, dogs, your breath, your body, the rain, the air are ALL MADE OF ATOMS.

The average ATOM can last a hundred

How big is an atom?

Atoms are pretty small. Half a million lined up in a row could hide behind a hair, and it takes 300 billion billion atoms to make one drop of water. To see the atoms in the water drop below, you'd need to enlarge the photo to 200 miles (320 km) wide.

What do atoms look like?

An atom doesn't look like anything. It's too small to reflect light, so the only object that makes any sense. Even so, it is possible to take pictures of the surface of solid objects and to see the clumps of round single atoms. The picture below shows a few of solid atoms (red and yellow on a flat surface, shown as unknown atoms (green on top).

How long do atoms last?

Atoms are almost indestructible. When you die, the atoms in your body don't die with you—they get recycled. About a billion of your atoms were once in the bodies of Julius Caesar, Jesus Christ, and Aristotle. Nobody knows for sure how long atoms can last, but one eminent scientist figures that 100,000,000,000,000,000,000,000,000,000,000 years is a sensible estimate.

You've got a billion bits of me in you!

Aristotle

made of?

Nearly every atom in your BODY was part of millions of other creatures before it got to YOU

million billion billion billion years

How were atoms discovered?

The first really good evidence for atoms came from the discovery that certain chemicals always combine in particular proportions (because the atoms join in ratios to make molecules). Later, scientists found they could explain the way pressure and temperature change in a gas if you assume the gas is made of billions of tiny particles that bounce.

Can you split atoms?

When scientists discovered atoms about 200 years ago, they thought atoms were the smallest bits of matter possible and therefore impossible to split. But atoms do split—just rub your hair and you'll split some. Splitting the middle part of an atom (the nucleus) is very difficult though. And it can cause a nuclear explosion.

What are molecules?

Atoms tend to stick together. They pull on each other with powerful forces and glue themselves into clumps called molecules. Water molecules (H₂O) are made of three atoms each—some large oxygen atom glued to two small hydrogen atoms. Nearly everything we see and touch is made of molecules.

What's *inside* an ATOM?

Deep inside an atom is a ZOO of even smaller particles. They inhabit a weird world where the normal laws of physics don't work.

ELECTRON

Electrons whizz around the nucleus, trapped by a pulling force from it. People once thought electrons orbited like planets round the Sun, but the truth is weirder. An electron is never really in one place at a time. It exists in lots of places at once as a sort of cloud of possibility. Weirder still, an electron can leap to a new orbit without passing through the space between—a "quantum leap."

NEUTRON

Neutrons are like protons but have no charge. In fact, a neutron can turn into a proton by spitting out an electron, which leaves it positive. Most atoms have about as many neutrons as protons, but big atoms have an excess of neutrons. The extra neutrons increase the strong nuclear force to hold all the protons together. If taken out of an atom, a neutron lasts 886 seconds and then falls apart.

NUCLEUS

The nucleus is the solid center of the atom, where nearly all the atom's weight is concentrated. It's surprisingly tiny, taking up only one millionth of a billionth of the space in the atom. If the whole atom were as big as a cathedral, the nucleus would be the size of a fly. Since electrons are even smaller (and in fact have zero size), an atom consists almost entirely of empty space.

QUARK

Each proton and neutron is made up of three even stranger particles called quarks. Quarks can't exist on their own—they only come in pairs or triplets. Sometimes, pairs of quarks emerge out of nothingness for no reason whatsoever. The strong nuclear force that holds the nucleus together is transmitted by pairs of quarks emerging from nothing and flying around.

PROTON

The nucleus is made of two types of particle: protons and neutrons. Protons have a positive charge that pulls on the electrons, which are negative. The nucleus can hold more than 100 protons, so why don't all these positive particles repel each other and blow the atom apart? The answer is that they're held together by a powerful force that only exists inside atomic nuclei: the strong nuclear force.

STRING

Imagine you shrank to the size of an atom, shrank by the same amount again, and then shrank by the same amount a third time. What would you see? According to the latest big theory, you'd see loops of "string." String theory says that all the particles in atoms are vibrations on the same kind of string, just as a violin string can create all the different musical notes.

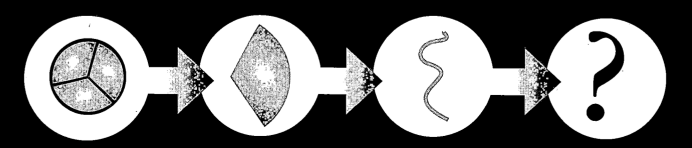

Why do *balloons* STICK to the wall?

FAQ

What happens when you switch on the light?

While balloons are good at trapping electrons, other substances—such as metals—let electrons flow through them. This is called current electricity. When you switch on a light, you connect two wires together and so let current electricity flow around a circuit. The moving electrons carry energy and power the bulb.

How fast do electrons flow?

People once thought electricity is like flowing water, but in reality it's more like a row of pool balls. If you hit the ball at the end, the force is passed along in a relay. In an wire, electrons nudge each other in a similar way. The electrons themselves move slower than a snail, but their energy zips through at the *speed of light*.

WHAT IS ELECTRICITY?

Electrons normally stay in atoms because they are held there by a FORCE. Electrons have a negative charge and the nuclei of atoms have a positive charge. Opposite charges pull on each other (a bit like opposite poles of a magnet), and like charges push each other away (they repel). Because electrons and nuclei have opposite charges, they pull on each other and stick together, forming atoms. But they don't always stay together. Sometimes electrons can break off atoms and carry their charge elsewhere, and that's what causes electricity.

Can you make your hair stand on end?

We normally think of electricity flowing through wires, but sometimes electrons get stuck in one place. When that happens, it causes something called *static electricity*. It's easy to create static electricity by rubbing objects together. If you rub your hair with a polyester T-shirt, the T-shirt will strip electrons from your hair. Your hairs become positively charged and repel each other, which makes them stand on end.

A brief *history* of ELECTRICITY

1700	1730	1752
The ancient Greeks had discovered static electricity in amber by 600 BC. Around 1700, scientists discovered how to build machines that create powerful sparks of static electricity.	English scientist Stephen Gray suspended a boy from a silk rope and charged him with static, proving that the human body can be charged like amber.	American statesman Benjamin Franklin flew a kite into a storm cloud to prove that lightning is caused by electricity. He coined the terms positive and negative charge (and got them the wrong way around.)

Rub a balloon on your hair and hold it to the wall. It will stick there, but what's holding it? It's the same thing that traps electrons around the nuclei of atoms: ELECTRICITY.

How do balloons stick to the wall?

Static electricity is what makes balloons stick to the wall after rubbing them on your hair. As you rub a balloon, electrons break off your hair and stick to the rubber, giving it a negative charge. When you press the balloon to the wall, the electrons push away electrons in the wall and make its surface positive. And so the negative balloon sticks to the positive wall surface.

Opposite charges *attract,*
similar charges *repel*

Why are carpets shocking?

The electrons trapped in static electricity will try to escape as soon as they touch something that lets them flow away. This can happen so quickly that it causes a spark or an electric shock. If you have shoes with plastic soles and walk on a nylon carpet, your body picks up electrons. When you touch something metal like a door handle, the charge rushes through you and gives you a shock.

FAQ

How does lightning work?

Lightning is caused by static electricity. Inside a storm cloud, ice crystals race up and down and rub each other. For unknown reasons, this makes electrons collect at the bottom of the cloud, making it negative. The charge is so vast that it forces its way to the ground by tearing the electrons off air atoms to create a charged path—a bolt of lightning.

How wide is a bolt of lightning?

A bolt of lightning is only 1 in (2–3 cm) wide but carries a huge amount of energy. Traveling at 270,000 mph (435,000 km/h), it heats the air to 50,400°F (28,000°C) and makes it explode, causing the bang we hear as thunder. Most bolts carry negative charge, but some positive bolts strike from cloud tops. They are deadlier and can be many miles long.

1753	1771	1800	1879	1897
Russian scientist George Richmann tried to repeat Franklin's experiment and was struck by lightning and killed.	Italian scientist Luigi Galvani discovered that frogs' legs twitch when given an electric shock, and concluded that electricity is the essence of life. The theory inspired the story of Frankenstein.	Alessandro Volta invented the battery after investigating Galvani's twitching frogs' legs.	After thousands of experiments, Thomas Edison perfected the light bulb.	English scientist J. J. Thomson discovered the electron in 1897—years after people had started using electric power.

Shocking experiments

Leaping men	Electric flea circus	Bending water

Draw a tiny outline of a man on thin paper and cut him out through several sheets of paper to make a group. Scatter the men on a table. Rub a balloon or CD box quickly on your hair for 30 seconds and then lower it over the men.

What's going on?
The balloon picks up electrons from your hair and becomes negative. As you lower it, the negative charge pushes away electrons in the paper men and makes their tops positive. Opposites attract, so the men leap up to the balloon.

Scatter mustard seeds, rice, or paper circles from a hole puncher on a sheet of paper. Rub the lid of a CD box on your hair for 30 seconds. Hold the lid a finger's height over the seeds and lower it very slowly. The seeds will dance up and down like jumping fleas.

What's going on?
The CD lid becomes negatively charged and pushes electrons in the seeds toward the bottom, making their tops positive. They jump up and stick to the lid, but their charge then seeps away and they drop off. The process repeats, making them dance up and down.

Turn on a cold faucet and slowly close it to make a smooth, thin stream of water. Rub a balloon or a plastic object on your hair to charge it with static. Hold the charged object near the water and watch what happens.

What's going on?
The balloon or plastic picks up electrons and becomes negative. When you hold it near the water, it repels electrons on the near side of the water, making that side of the water positive. The positive side is drawn toward the balloon, making the stream of water bend.

POSITIVE THIS END

Some materials are good at giving away electrons and becoming positive when you rub them, but others are better at taking electrons and becoming negative.

Skin | Rabbit fur | Glass | Hair | Nylon | Wool | Cat fur | Silk | Paper | Cotton (neutral)

Shock your family, friends, and yourself with these ELECTRIFYING experiments! Most of them work best when the air is very dry—a sunny winter's day is perfect. In humid or wet weather, moisture in the air makes static electricity seep away. Tip: make sure you hair is clean and dry.

Sour power

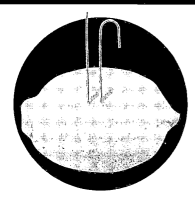

Gently squeeze a lemon, then stab it with a straightened paper clip and an equal length of copper wire, placed close together. (Ask an adult to strip an old cable to make the copper wire.) Press your tongue to both at once and you'll feel a tingling sensation.

What's going on?
The lemon is a battery. Acid inside it reacts chemically with both metals. Electrons leak away from the copper (making it positive) and build up on the paper clip (making it negative). When you lick the wires you complete the circuit and the charge flows across your tongue.

Snake charmer

Draw a spiral pattern on a piece of lightweight paper and cut along the line. Rub a plastic pen vigorously on your hair or your jumper for 30 seconds. Hold the pen near the middle of the spiral and slowly lift it.

What's going on?
The pen picks up electrons from your hair and becomes negatively charged. When you hold it to the paper, it repels electrons. The paper then becomes positive and sticks to the pen, rising as you lift it—just like a snake being charmed!

Sparks in the dark

1. Fully extend the antenna on a radio (not a digital one). Charge a balloon on your sweater and check it sticks to your sweater. Now slowly bring it toward the antenna and listen. What do you hear? Does the balloon still stick to your sweater?
2. Switch on the radio, set it to AM or medium wave and tune it away from a station. Turn the volume to full. Charge the balloon and bring it slowly to the antenna again. What do you hear?
3. With the room in total darkness, charge the balloon and touch the antenna one more time. What do you see?

ANSWERS
1. You hear a crack as the electrons leap to the antenna. The balloon no longer sticks to your sweater because the charge has gone.
2. You hear a much louder pop because the radio picks up the spark and turns it into sound.
3. You see tiny sparks as the charge leaps through the air—lightning in miniature.

When arranged in order, these materials make what scientists call the "triboelectric series." To generate a good static electric charge, rub things from opposite ends of the series together.

NEGATIVE THIS END

| Steel (neutral) | Wood | Amber | Rubber | Brass | Gold | Polyester | Polystyrene | Polythene | Clingfilm (PVC) |

FAQ

[The FAQ section text is too faded and low-resolution to read reliably.]

How do *MAGNETS*

The electrons that whizz around ATOMS don't just create electricity. They are also responsible for the *mysterious force* of magnetism.

Magnets are surrounded by something called a *field of force*. It's invisible, but you can see it by scattering iron filings on a piece of paper and placing a magnet on top. The iron filings jiggle around until they align with the magnet's field. They also cluster around the poles, where the magnetic force is strongest.

work?

Whenever an ELECTRON moves, it creates a magnetic field around it just like the field around a bar magnet. Every atom has electrons, so every atom is magnetic. Normally the atomic magnets in objects are mixed up and their force fields cancel each other out. However, in some materials, like iron, the magnetic fields of atoms can line up together. Then the whole piece of iron acts as one magnet.

FAQ

Can electricity make magnetism?

Although magnetism and electricity seem like very different things, they are actually different aspects of the same force: *electromagnetism*. The first inkling of a link came in 1802, when an Italian scientist discovered by accident that electric wires can swing compass needles round. The moving electrons in the wire were creating a magnetic field. The English scientist Michael Faraday went on to discover that the opposite can happen too: if you move a magnet next to a wire, the moving magnetic field generates electricity. Faraday had invented a way of creating electricity from movement. It was one the greatest scientific inventions ever, and today we get nearly all our electricity this way.

Make a compass

If you have a strong magnet, you can use it to make a compass. Stroke a steel needle with the magnet in one direction only for 15 seconds. Tape the needle to a piece of cork or styrofoam and float it in water. The needle will turn round to point north.

What makes the best magnets?

Neodymium magnets, which are made from a mixture of iron, boron, and neodymium, are up to 20 times more powerful than normal iron magnets. There are tiny neodymium magnets in ear phones—if you have a pair, try picking up paper clips or pins with them. A neodymium magnet the size of a penny can lift a 20 lb (10 kg) weight and will pick up metal objects through your hand.

When the same poles of two magnets are pushed together, they repel each other. The field is weak between them and the lines of force curve away.

When opposite poles of two magnets are put together, they pull each other strongly. The force field is strong, and lines of force run between the magnets.

There are three ways that heat can move around:

CONDUCTION:

Molecules transfer their energy as they bounce into each other. When you hold a hot cup of coffee, heat enters your hand by conduction.

CONVECTION:

When air gets hot, it expands and becomes lighter. As a result it floats upward, taking the heat energy with it.

RADIATION:

Hot objects give off heat as invisible rays, called infrared rays. You can feel the Sun's infrared rays as warmth on your skin.

FAQ

Why is metal cold and wood warm?

Metal often feels colder than wood, even when they are the same temperature. Why the difference? Metals are far better at *conducting* heat. They conduct heat away from your hand, cooling your skin.

How can you trap heat?

Materials that are bad at conducting heat are good at holding it in, or *insulating*. Clothes that trap lots of air are good at keeping you warm because air is a very poor conductor.

Can you feel the *heat?*

Imagine you had a powerful microscope that could zoom in to look at atoms and molecules.

You'd see the atoms and molecules jiggling around.

We feel this jiggling motion as HEAT. The faster the atoms jiggle, the hotter they feel. *Temperature* is just a measure of how FAST the jiggling atoms are moving.

Surface of the Sun

10,800°F (6,000°C)

Iron melts

5,182°F (2,861°C)

2,800°F (1,538°C)

Water boils

446°F (230°C)

212°F (100°C)

Iron boils

Paper catches fire

Can you see heat?

Although infrared rays are invisible to our eyes, special cameras can detect them and take "heat pictures," or thermograms. This thermogram of a plate of spaghetti shows hot areas as red and white but cold areas as blue.

What has more heat—an iceberg or a cup of coffee?

The temperature of an object tells you how fast its atoms are moving, but not how much heat energy it has altogether. A cup of coffee has a higher temperture than an iceberg, but the iceberg has more heat because it has many times more atoms.

Make a heat engine

This cunning device turns heat energy into motion. Cut out a piece of paper in the shape shown below (but larger). Fold along the dotted line, then balance it on the sharpened point of a pencil. Stand the pencil in modeling clay for support. Rub your hands as hard as you can for 10 seconds to create heat from friction, then hold your hands under the paper. Hot air will rise by convection and blow the fan round.

Hottest weather on Earth

136°F (58°C)

Water freezes

32°F (0°C)

Mercury freezes

−38°F (−39°C)

Coldest weather on Earth

−128°F (−89°C)

Air becomes liquid

−321°F (−196°C)

Air freezes

−362°F (−219°C)

−454°F (−270°C)

Outer space

Absolute zero

−459°F (−273°C)

Absolute zero...

is the lowest temperature possible, when atoms have no kinetic energy and stop moving. Actually, it's impossible to get all the way down to absolute zero, but you can get close. Weird things happen within a millionth of a degree of absolute zero. Atoms lose their individuality and slide into each other, forming a single atom-sized blob—a "Bose-Einstein condensate."

States of matter

Solid

MELT
As a solid heats up, its atoms move faster. Eventually they get fast enough to break their ties and separate.

FREEZE
As a liquid cools, the atoms lose energy and slow down, until they lock together in a solid.

Liquid

Cool or squeeze liquids to make solids

ALTERED STATES

Breaking the rules
Some substances, like glass, are permanently in between solid and liquid. As glass gets hotter it gets runnier. As it cools it gets harder, but it never *completely* sets. Even solid glass flows slowly over millions of years.

Glass sculpture

Hot glass

The fourth state
If you make a gas *really* hot you'll end up with a fourth state of matter: PLASMA. In plasma the electrons are torn free from atoms, so plasma can conduct electricity. Lightning is made of plasma. So are the Sun and stars, which makes plasma the most common state of matter in the universe.

Plasma globe

Boil a glass of water until it *disappears* and you'll make enough steam to fill a room. Steam is water blown apart into a cloud, just as ice is water frozen tight into a block. Like ice, water, and steam, all matter can exist in three states: SOLID, LIQUID, and GAS. But these aren't the only states...

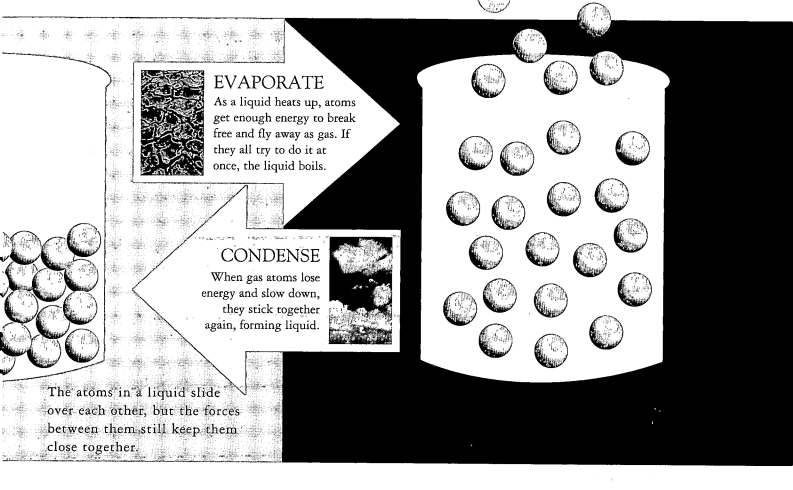

EVAPORATE
As a liquid heats up, atoms get enough energy to break free and fly away as gas. If they all try to do it at once, the liquid boils.

CONDENSE
When gas atoms lose energy and slow down, they stick together again, forming liquid.

The atoms in a liquid slide over each other, but the forces between them still keep them close together.

Heat or stretch liquids to make gases

Neon signs use plasma to produce light.

Star matter
Solids, liquids, gases, and plasma are not the only states of matter. In a neutron star, atoms are crushed so tight that they disintegrate into a sea of neutrons—a gigantic atomic nucleus several miles (km) wide, with gravity a trillion times stronger than Earth's.

WHAT *shape is a*

Water is an amazing substance that covers 70 percent of Earth's surface. What makes it so special are its *molecules*. Each one has two tiny hydrogen atoms joined to one oxygen atom. This gives them a positive electrical charge at one end and a negative charge at the other. So they SNAP TOGETHER and stick to things like tiny magnets.

$$+ \quad + \quad = \quad H_2O$$

2 HYDROGEN ATOMS   1 OXYGEN ATOM

What shape is a raindrop?
Raindrops are not teardrop-shaped as people suppose but ball-shaped. Inside a drop, water molecules are pulled in all directions by the electrical forces between them. But at the surface, the molecules are only pulled inward. The inward pull tugs the droplet into a *sphere*. Tiny drops are almost perfectly spherical, but big drops flatten on the wind as they fall and become bun-shaped.

Can you walk on water?
Because water molecules on the surface of a pond can't pull on any molecules above them, their pulling forces are concentrated in the surface layer. The result is a tight, stretchy skin on the surface, which is strong enough for insects to walk on. This is called surface tension.

raindrop?

Why do icebergs float?

Most liquids get more compact as they freeze, but water is the opposite. Its molecules spread out as they solidify, making water expand by about 10 percent as it freezes. As a result, ice is lighter than water and floats rather than sinking. With ice on the top, water underneath can stay warmer. This helps life survive in lakes and rivers in winter.

As water freezes into ice crystals, the molecules form an orderly pattern similar to the pattern of atoms in diamonds.

Float a paper clip

You can float a paper clip on water if you're careful. Place the paper clip on a fork and lower it very slowly into the water. The paper clip will be held by the stretchy skin of the water. Touch the water with a soapy finger to destroy the surface tension and make the paper clip fall.

AIR   WATER

Unpoppable balloon

Water can soak up and store heat better than almost any other substance. You can see its amazing heat-absorbing ability with this trick. Fill one balloon with air and another with water. Hold a candle beneath each one and see what happens. The air balloon heats up quickly and pops, but the water balloon survives much longer.

It takes lots of energy to break the bonds that hold water molecules together. This is why water takes a long time to get hot.

69

CAN YOU *walk on*

Some fluids are thin

and fast-flowing, like water, but others are thick and slow, like honey. We call these thick fluids VISCOUS.

Stir a glass of water and it stays just as thin; stir a jar of syrup and it stays just as thick. This is how Isaac Newton thought all fluids should work, but there are some—such as custard and ketchup—that don't obey his rules. If you stir or shake them, the FORCE you apply changes their inner structure and makes them either runnier or more viscous. Fluids like this are called *non-Newtonian*.

> *Non-Newtonian?*
> How very dare you!

How does quicksand work?

Quicksand is a soupy mixture of sand and water that sometimes forms on beaches, riverbanks, over springs, or in marshes. It can look solid to the touch, but when you step on it you quickly sink in. Then, as you struggle to free yourself, the force of your movements makes the quicksand more viscous. Sand collects in a dense mass around your legs, *trapping* you.

How to sink

The worst thing to do in quicksand is to panic and struggle. Thrashing your arms and legs around not only makes the fluid thicken like cement, but also digs you in deeper. And the deeper you sink, the harder it is to get out.

How to swim

The secret to escaping is to stay perfectly still. The fluid then becomes less viscous and you automatically float to the surface, since quicksand is much more dense (and therefore easier to float in) than water.

Can you walk on custard?

Cornstarch custard is a non-Newtonian fluid. If you apply a force to it, it turns solid. But does it harden enough to support the weight of a human being? In 2003, a team of researchers from the British TV program *Brainiac* decided to find out by filling a swimming pool with custard...

CUSTARD?

Why do you have to shake ketchup?

Ketchup is the opposite of quicksand—it gets runnier when you apply a force, which is why you have to shake the bottle to make it flow. Inside the bottle, ketchup is a mix of solids and liquids held together by a kind of invisible scaffolding. When you shake it, the force smashes the scaffolding and the ketchup becomes less viscous.

Tip: put the lid on before you shake it.

Toothpaste

The technical term for liquids that become less viscous when you apply a force is ***thixotropic***. Toothpaste is also thixotropic. Take the cap off and it just sits there, peering at you from the nozzle. Start squeezing and the force breaks up its structure and makes it squish out.

Make slime!

A good way to learn about non-Newtonian fluids is to make *slime* and explore its amazing properties. The recipe below tells you how to make cornstarch slime, which is runny when you leave it alone but becomes so viscous when you apply a force that it TURNS SOLID!

Put 1½ cups of cornstarch in a mixing bowl. Slowly mix in a cup or so of water, adding a little at a time and stirring. Add green food coloring to make the slime look like snot. Take a handful of slime and slap or squeeze it suddenly—it will turn solid. Let it relax a few seconds and it will become liquid and will ooze beween your fingers.

Custard does support the weight of a human being, but only if you keep moving. The impact of each step hardens the custard below, which then forms a firm support. However, if you stop walking, the custard liquefies again and you slowly sink in.

HOW *does* a *balloon* BURST?

Ever wondered why balloons are so hard to blow up but so easy to burst? The physics of air and rubber has the answers.

Why do balloons stretch?

The secret to the stretchiness of balloons is in the molecules. Balloons are made of rubber, which has long, thin molecules like strands of cooked spaghetti. When you stretch rubber, the strands slide over each other and straighten out. When you let go, tiny forces between the molecules pull them back into a tangled clump.

NORMAL

STRETCHED

Why does it *BANG*?

A balloon takes a fraction of a second to burst. As it collapses, bits of rubber snap back to their original shape at more than twice the speed of sound and the air rushes out in a shockwave that you hear as a loud bang, like the crack of a whip.

Why is it hard to blow up?

It takes a lot of effort to blow up a balloon because you have to overcome the forces trying to pull the rubber molecules back together. The first breath is hardest because you have to straighten out billions of rubber molecules at once. After that, the molecules slide past each other a little more easily as the rubber stretches, but they're still trying to pull themselves back. If you let go, the balloon will shrink suddenly and push out all the air. And that will make it fly out of your hand—a nifty demonstration of Newton's third law.

Can you pierce a balloon without bursting it?

Yes. If a balloon isn't overinflated, the rubber near the knot and around the top isn't fully stretched and will look thick and dark. Put a little grease or lip balm on the end of a skewer or a paper clip and gently push it into the dark rubber, twisting it until it pierces. With practice you can push a skewer right through both ends of the balloon.

What if you pierce it somewhere else?

Elsewhere the rubber is very taut. It's reached its "elastic limit," which means it will crack rather than stretch if the strain increases. Once tiny cracks appear, the pressurized air rushes out. Huge cracks race around the surface and the balloon bursts!

Balloon in a bottle

Here's a trick to baffle your friends. Show them an inflated balloon inside a bottle and challenge them to put their own balloon in another bottle and inflate it. When they try, the balloon will block the neck of the bottle and won't expand.

Here's the secret: put a straw in the bottle at the same time to let air escape as you blow up the balloon.

warm air

How does a balloon stay inflated?

Once you tie the knot, your breath is trapped in the balloon. A full balloon contains about 30,000 billion billion air molecules. Each one flies around at about 1,000 mph (1,600 km/h) and bounces into other molecules or the wall of the balloon 5 billion times a second. The millions of billions of collisions with the rubber press against it, and this pressure keeps the balloon inflated.

What if you put a balloon in the fridge?

Try it. Stick a balloon in the fridge and see what happens. After about an hour, the air molecules will by flying about 30 mph (50 km/h) slower and will hit the rubber with less force. But the force pulling the rubber molecules together will be just as strong, so the balloon will shrink until the forces balance again. If you warm the balloon on a radiator, the opposite happens and the balloon expands.

cold air

In a chilled balloon the air molecules move more slowly and hit the rubber with less force, so the balloon shrinks.

Can you *see* the LIGHT?

We all know that light is important—you wouldn't be able to read this page without it. You probably know that it's pretty quick too. Moving at a nifty 670 MILLION mph (1 BILLION km/h), *it's the fastest thing in the universe.*

But did you know that light could hold the secret to time travel? And it's impressively tricky stuff, sometimes acting as tiny particles and sometimes as ripples through the air, like radio waves.

IN FACT, LIGHT RAISES A LOT OF QUESTIONS. **How does it work?** Why do stars twinkle? *Why are sunsets red?* **And why did light cause the usually very intelligent Isaac Newton to stick a knitting needle in his eye?** Take advantage of the light around you right now to read on and find out.

PARTICLES

Is light made of *particles?*

Light is a riddle. It's the fastest thing in the universe and weighs absolutely nothing. We see it all the time, but we can't see what it's made of. Sometimes it acts like billions of tiny particles flying past at amazing speed. At other times it seems like a wave that ripples through the air. So what is light actually made of?

Bouncy balls

Isaac Newton was one of the first scientists to think of light as particles. If it was a wave, he thought, it wouldn't always travel in straight lines and make sharp shadows—it would flow around objects the way ocean waves wash around rocks and sound waves bend through doorways. Newton also saw that light bounces off mirrors just as balls bounce off a wall, which made him think light must be made of tiny bouncy particles.

Lost in space

The particle theory seemed to explain how light could travel to Earth from the Sun. Particles can fly across empty space, but waves need something to ripple in. Sound waves are ripples in air, for instance, and ocean waves are ripples on water. If light were a wave, what was doing the rippling as it passed through outer space?

The mighty atom

After scientists discovered how atoms work, they found that an atom can spit out light particles one at a time. This proved that light really is made of particles, and they were named **photons**.

Is light made of Waves?

The answer to the riddle is that light is both things at once: a wave and a particle. It just depends on how you look at it. It isn't just light that has this peculiar ability to be two things at once. All the tiny particles in atoms and even atoms themselves can act like particles or waves, depending on the circumstances.

Bendable light

The first inkling that light is a wave came from an Italian scientist called Grimaldi nearly 400 years ago. He made shadows with narrow beams of light and discovered that the shadows were slightly wider than they ought to be, as though the light had bent like a wave.

Ripples

Proof came about 200 years later. An English scientist called Thomas Young shone light through a grid of narrow slits. The light not only bent but formed ripply patterns similar to the patterns you see in a pond when two sets of ripples overlap. Young even worked out the length of the waves—they were less than a millionth of a meter.

Across the universe

The wave theory explained why colors exist (each color has a particular wavelength), but how could light waves travel in space? Scientists first thought space must be full of some invisible substance called "ether," but the true answer was much stranger. Empty space can contain invisible "force fields" exactly like the magnetic field around a magnet. Light is a ripple in these force fields.

WAVES

How do we see color?

Our eyes contain three types of color detector: one for red, one for green, and a third for blue. By combining them, we see every shade of color. It's a clever system but it's easily fooled. A TV tricks you into seeing colors that aren't there. To make yellow, for instance, it mixes tiny green and red lights, triggering the same combination of cells in your eyes that yellow light would trigger.

Rainbows

happen when the Sun is behind you and rain is falling in front. Sunlight enters each raindrop, bounces inside, and flies back out the front, spreading into colors like light from a prism. Rainbows are arched because you only see colors where light hits at a certain angle. If the ground wasn't in the way, the rainbow would be a circle.

When colors are arranged in order of wavelength, they make a pattern called a *spectrum*. The spectrum has seven main bands that blend into each other gradually, creating countless different colors. The human eye can see as many as **10 million** colors, including some that aren't in the spectrum at all, such as brown and magenta.

What *color is*

Light that looks white

is really a mixture of every different color, jumbled together so thoroughly that you can't see any of them separately. When sunlight shines through raindrops or bounces off the back of a CD, the hidden colors fly apart and reveal themselves in rainbow patterns.

Why do colors exist? Colors exist because light waves can be different lengths.

If the waves are LONG, we see them as red.

If the waves are SHORT, we see them as blue.

Light waves are very short, even in red light. About 2,000 waves stretching end-to-end would fit along a millimeter.

Learn this phrase to *remember*

RED **O**RANGE **Y**ELLOW

Richard *of* *York*

LIGHT?

Who discovered the colors in light?

On a sunny day in 1665, when Isaac Newton was only 22, he shut himself in a darkened room in his mother's farmhouse in England. He let a sliver of light through a chink in the curtains and put a triangular wedge of glass—a "prism"—in the beam of light. The beam spread out into a spectrum of colors. Scientists already knew about this beautiful effect, but they thought the colors came from the glass. Newton proved otherwise. He put a second prism in the spectrum and focused the rays back together. Lo and behold, a spot of white light appeared on the wall.

Within weeks of his discovery, Newton was *famous.*

Sight for sore Isaac

Spurred on by his success with prisms, Newton conducted more experiments. One was very stupid. Newton thought the human eye might work like a prism, splitting light into the colors we see. To test this theory, he shoved a knitting needle into the back of his eye and squidged his eyeball to see if colors appeared. They didn't. The theory was wrong, and Newton ended up with a nasty eye infection that nearly blinded him.

Why do diamonds sparkle?

Diamonds can split white light into colors even more effectively than a glass prism can. A well-cut diamond also makes the light bounce around inside. That's why diamonds sparkle with brilliant, fiery colors.

Make a spectrum

You can make a spectrum with a glass of water. Cut a very thin slit in some cardboard and tape it to the glass. Stand the glass on a sheet of paper by a sunny window so light shines through the slit. As the white light crosses the water surface, it will bend and split to form a spectrum.

Add colors together

You can add colors together by making a color wheel. Use paint or a computer to create a colored disk like the one below. Glue the disk to cardboard, push a sharp pencil through the middle, and spin it. If you get the color combination just right the disk will turn white!

the order of colors of the spectrum

GREEN BLUE INDIGO VIOLET

gave battle in vain

Can you see rainbows in *bubbles?*

A bubble is

like a balloon of air, but its skin is a film of liquid rather than rubber. The film has three layers: an inner and an outer layer of soap molecules, and a layer of water molecules sandwiched between. The water molecules pull on each other, creating a force called surface tension, which holds the bubble together. The film is less than a thousandth of a millimeter thick, which is about the same as the wavelength of light.

When light

waves reflect off a bubble, they crash together and interfere. You can see a similar effect by throwing pebbles in a pond. One pebble makes a set of circular waves that spread out neatly, but two pebbles make two sets of waves that interfere. Where the peaks of two waves combine, they make a bigger wave. If a peak of one wave joins with the valley of another, the two waves cancel each other out. Light waves do the same.

The colors on a bubble keep changing as the soap and water swirl around. As the thickness of the film varies, different colors are reflected. If you blow gently on a bubble, the skin gets thinner and the color changes from green to blue to pink to yellow. Then the colors vanish and the bubble bursts.

Peer at a soap bubble and you'll see rainbow colors swirling all over it. If you blow on the bubble the colors will spin and change...

... but where do the *colors* come from?

Light reflects

off the inner and outer surfaces of a bubble film, making two sets of waves that interfere. Where the bubble's skin is just thick enough, certain wavelengths bounce back in step. Those are the colors you see. Other wavelengths bounce back out of step and cancel out, so those colors disappear.

white light

green waves in step

white light

red waves cancel out

NOW TRY THIS!

plastic

Make a **bubbularium** to light up bubbles from inside! Tape some clear, stiff plastic to a flashlight. Put a spoonful of bubble liquid on the plastic and use a straw to blow bubbles in it. Switch off the lights, turn on the flashlight, and hold the bubbularium above eye level.

Tip: add gelatin or sugar to the bubble liquid to make stronger bubbles with brighter colors.

When is light invisible?

Suppose you used a pair of tweezers to stretch waves of light. As the waves got longer, they'd change color. Then they'd become **invisible**, because our eyes can only see certain wavelengths. There are many types of light with wavelengths too long or short for us to see. Along with visible light, they make up the vast "electromagnetic spectrum."

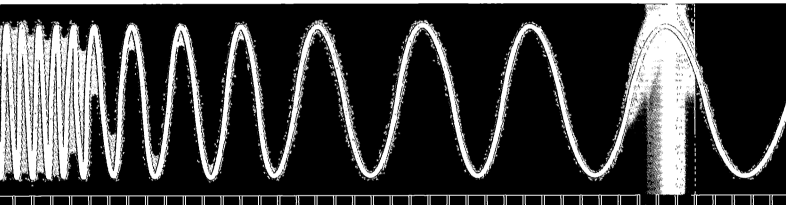

Gamma rays   X-rays   Ultraviolet   Visible

Gamma rays are the most dangerous electromagnetic rays. Their waves are even smaller than atoms but are packed with energy and can zip right through solid objects and kill living cells. They are given off by nuclear bombs as "radioactivity" and are used to destroy cancer.

X-ray waves are about the size of atoms and contain lots of energy, but are less harmful than gamma rays. They pass through most parts of the human body but are blocked by bones, teeth, and metal, which makes them ideal for seeing inside things.

Ultraviolet (UV) rays come from the Sun but we can't see them, though bees, birds, and butterflies can. Some wavelengths of UV light can pass deep into human skin and damage the living cells inside, causing sunburn, cancer, or wrinkles that make people look old.

Visible light is the only type of electromagnetic radiation that our eyes can detect. It comes in a range of wavelengths, which we see as colors. These wavelengths are ideal for vision because sunlight is full of them and they bounce off objects rather than passing through.

wavelength

Are you receiving me?

The world is full of electromagnetic rays that you can't see or feel. Unless the waves are just the right size to interact with atoms, they pass through objects like light going through a window. Every second, hundreds of TV programs and thousands of phone calls pass right through your body as invisible radio waves.

Infrared   Microwave   Radio   Radio

Infrared rays carry heat. Although they're invisible, you can see them if you wear night-vision goggles, and you can feel them on your skin when you warm your hands by a fire. Infrared waves vary in size from microscopically tiny to the size of a pinhead.

Microwaves are very short radio waves. They vary from the size of a pinhead to the length of your arm. Microwave ovens flood food with waves about 5 in (12 cm) long. These wavelengths heat up water molecules but pass through things like glass and plastic.

Cell phones and Wi-Fi gadgets send their signals as short radio waves, which vary from the size of microwaves to a few yards (meters) long. Short radio waves travel best in straight lines and don't bend around obstacles well.

TV and radio stations broadcast in longer radio waves, from a few yards (meters) long (TV and FM radio) to hundreds of yards (AM radio). Very long waves bend around obstacles and curve through the atmosphere, which allows them to travel around the world.

Why is the sky BLUE?

The *color* of the sky comes from the *air*, which looks blue when sunlight hits it. If you were on the Moon, which has no air, the sky would be jet black. Earth, however, is covered by a thin blanket of air—the **atmosphere**.

When sunlight reaches Earth after its long journey from the Sun, it passes through the atmosphere. Remember that white sunlight is actually a mixture of all the colors of the rainbow. Some colors, such as red, cut straight through air without a problem. But other colors—particularly blue—crash into air molecules and bounce off in new directions. When you look up, you see this scattered light as a blue glow coming from the air.

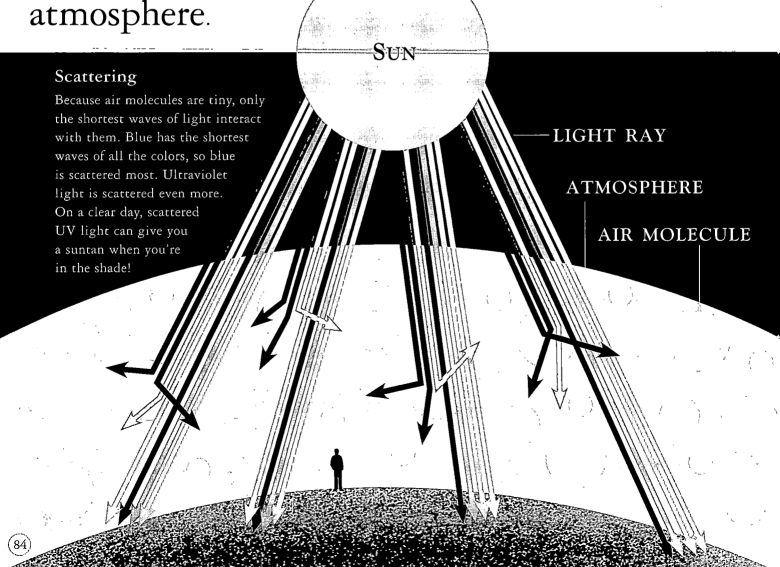

Scattering

Because air molecules are tiny, only the shortest waves of light interact with them. Blue has the shortest waves of all the colors, so blue is scattered most. Ultraviolet light is scattered even more. On a clear day, scattered UV light can give you a suntan when you're in the shade!

SUN

——LIGHT RAY

ATMOSPHERE

AIR MOLECULE

Water droplet

Why are clouds white?
It's not just air molecules that scatter light. The water droplets in clouds scatter light too, but they are much bigger than air molecules and so can scatter long as well as short wavelengths. Since all the different wavelengths add up to make white, the light we see from clouds is white.

Why are sunsets red?
As the Sun sinks at the end of the day, its light has to travel through a thicker and thicker slice of the atmosphere. The air scatters more and more of the short wavelengths away, leaving just long wavelengths like red and orange. And that's why sunsets are red. Very fine dust, such as salt particles over the sea or ash from volcanoes, can make the sunset even redder.

Midday Sun overhead

More air to travel through

Why is the sea blue?
A glass of water is colorless, but water in the sea is deep blue on a sunny day. The color of water is caused by a process different from scattering. Water absorbs long wavelengths of light, such as red, but lets short wavelengths like blue pass through and bounce around. So light that passes through water is blue. In very deep water the blue is absorbed too and the sea turns black.

How *fast* is
light?

Light is the **fastest** thing in the universe. It travels at about 670 million mph (1 billion km/h), which is 10 million times faster than the highway speed limit and 40,000 times faster than the Space Shuttle. At that speed, a beam of light can zip around the world *seven* times in just one second.

Why is light weird?

According to the laws of physics, light behaves oddly. Say you're chasing a car that's going 20 mph (32 km/h). If you ran behind it at 19 mph (30.4 km/h), the car would be going 1 mile (1.6 km/h) faster. You could almost keep up. The weird thing is, this doesn't happen with light. No matter how fast you chase light, it always moves away at exactly the same speed. Even if Superman were flying at 669,999,999 mph (999,999,999 km/h) behind a beam of light, the light would still speed away from him at 670 million mph (1 billion km/h). He might as well be *standing still*.

Surely that's impossible?

No. The first person to realize that light really does travel in what seems an impossible way was Albert Einstein. Einstein figured out that if light doesn't change its relative speed, then time and space must be shrinking and stretching to make up for it. That means that as Superman gets close to the speed of light, his body shrinks and time slows down.

Can light slow down?

Light only reaches its top speed in the emptiness of space. If something gets in the way—like air, water, or glass—it slows down. The sudden change of speed also bends light, and this is why straight objects placed in water often look crooked. The bending effect is called **refraction**. If it didn't happen, we couldn't make telescopes, cameras, magnifying glasses, or eyeglasses.

Albert Einstein
(1879–1955)

Can you *travel*

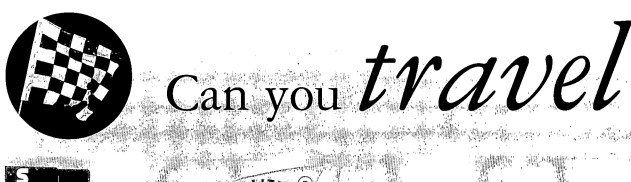

1% *of light speed*

Imagine you're in a race car that can go as fast as you like. Your challenge is to reach the speed of light and see what happens. You step on the accelerator and push the speed up to 6.7 million mph (10 million km/h)—just 1% of light speed. So far, things seem pretty normal. So you put your foot down and speed up some more...

Space bends

Einstein's theory is called the theory of relativity because how things look depends on how you're moving relative to them. In the world of relativity, gravity is different too. We usually think of gravity as a force that tugs things to the Earth, but in Einstein's theory gravity happens for another reason. Heavy objects—like planet Earth—*bend space and time*. This is easier to understand if you imagine space and time as a sheet of stretchy rubber. If you put planet Earth in the middle, it makes a dip. Now roll the Moon past. It follows the curve of space and gets trapped in orbit around Earth because it can't climb out of the dip.

What you *see* depends on how

at the speed of light?

90%   99%   99.99%

... Now you're doing 90% of light speed and things are getting weird. e people outside, your car has shortened to half its length and time has slowed down inside your car. From your point of view, the spectators have become narrower and slower, and your car seems fine.

At 99 percent of light speed, your car is less than a yard (meter) long, you're seven times heavier, and a day for you lasts a week to the people outside. They now look as thin as rakes and are moving in slow motion. When they speak, their words come out increddddddibly slowwwwwly.

At 99.99% of light speed, your car is shorter than a pencil and a second lasts more than a minute. Going faster just makes you shorter and slows time even more. You can never reach the speed of light—it's impossible. If you could, you'd be zero length, heavier than the universe, and time would stop.

Gravity changes time

Einstein discovered that gravity slows down time. At the top of a mountain, where Earth's gravity is very slightly weaker, time runs a little quicker. But only a *tiny bit* quicker. Even if you spent your entire life at the summit of Mount Everest, you'd get older by only a tiny fraction of a second more than your friends at sea level.

Time travel

According to Einstein, traveling forward in time is easy. Jump in a rocket, whizz around the universe at 99.99% of the speed of light (or hang around something with colossal gravity, like a black hole), and come back in 4 months. Everyone you know will be 24 years older!

you're moving—that's RELATIVITY

Who's who?

The brilliant scientist and mathematician Sir Isaac Newton once said, "If I have seen farther, it was by standing on the shoulders of giants." Newton meant that his own work was built on the work of the great scientists who lived before him. Here are some of the biggest names in physics, starting in ancient Greece.

All men by nature desire knowledge

ARISTOTLE 384–322 BC	ARCHIMEDES 287–212 BC	COPERNICUS 1473–1543	GILBERT 1544–1603
One of the great thinkers of the ancient world, the Greek philosopher Aristotle was an expert on subjects from anatomy and astronomy to physics and philosophy. He was a tutor to Alexander the Great and a lecturer at the greatest school in Greece. He valued knowledge gained from observing nature and said, "Nature does nothing uselessly."	A Greek mathematician, astronomer, physicist, and engineer, Archimedes invented war machines and a device to lift water uphill. His most famous moment (when he sprang out of the bath shouting "Eureka!") came when he discovered that the king's crown wasn't solid gold, because it displaced more water than the same weight of pure gold.	The Polish astronomer Nicolas Copernicus believed that the Sun, not the Earth, is the center of the universe, and that the planets revolve around the Sun. Although this idea offended the ruling Catholic Church, his work helped later scientists unravel the forces that govern the universe, and it formed the basis of modern astronomy.	A distinguished London doctor (and physician to Elizabeth I), William Gilbert is best known for his research into electricity and magnetism. In his book *De Magnete* (*On Magnetism*), he explained how magnets attract and repel. He also showed that Earth is like a giant bar magnet, which is why a compass needle always points north.

> **All truths are easy to understand once they are discovered; the point is to discover them**

> **If I have ever made any valuable discoveries, it has been owing more to patient attention than to any other talent**

GALILEO 1564–1642	NEWTON 1642–1727	FRANKLIN 1706–1790	VOLTA 1745–1827

The Italian scientist Galileo Galilei used a telescope of his own design to study the Moon, Sun, stars, and to discover Jupiter's moons. He rolled balls down ramps in experiments on gravity and discovered that all falling objects accelerate at the same rate. His views on astronomy led the Church to place him under house arrest for the last years of his life.

The English scientist Isaac Newton often tops polls as the greatest scientist ever, but he had strange religious ideas and believed in alchemy (a magical form of chemistry). Best known for figuring out how gravity holds the universe together, he also published theories of color. He was very sensitive to criticism and fell out with many of his contemporaries.

One of the founding fathers of America, Benjamin Franklin was a prominent politician and diplomat as well as a scientist. He discovered that lightning is a form of electricity by flying a kite in a storm, and he invented the lightning conductor. He was the first person to describe electricity as having positive and negative forms.

Italian physicist Alessandro Volta did not speak until he was four but soon caught up with his classmates. He invented the first battery by discovering that an electric current could flow between two metals in a solution. His fame spread and he performed experiments in front of Napoleon. The basic unit of electric force was named the volt in his honor.

Volta's battery

> *Nothing is too wonderful to be true if it be consistent with the laws of nature*

> *One never notices what has been done; one can only see what remains to be done*

> If the facts don't fit the theory, change the facts

FARADAY 1791–1867	MAXWELL 1831–1879	CURIE 1867–1934	EINSTEIN 1879–1955
The English physicist Michael Faraday was a brilliant experimenter. He discovered that electricity and magnetism are closely linked and he built the first electrical generator. An enthusiastic public speaker, he founded the tradition of Christmas science lectures that continues at England's Royal Institution to this day.	Nicknamed Dafty as a boy, James Clerk Maxwell of Scotland grew up to be a brilliant physicist, famous for summing up electro-magnetism in four short equations. He showed that electricity and magnetism can travel as waves and he proved that light is a form of electromagnetic radiation. He also showed that heating a gas makes the atoms move faster.	The first female Nobel prize winner, Polish-born Marie Curie is famous for her work on radioactivity. She discovered two radioactive elements and worked out how to purify one of them (radium). The discoveries led to a new treatment for cancer: radiotherapy. Ironically, Marie Curie died of a type of cancer caused by exposure to radioactivity.	Albert Einstein's first success was to show that light is made of particles (photons), but he is better known for his theory of relativity, which links space, time, and gravity with the speed of light. His formula $E = mc^2$ shows that energy and mass are the same thing. Einstein opposed war, but his work led to the invention of nuclear bombs, which convert mass into energy.

> *All science is either physics or stamp collecting*

> What we observe as material bodies and forces are nothing but shapes and variations in the structure of space

> In science one tries to tell people, in such a way as to be understood by everyone, something that no one ever knew before

RUTHERFORD 1871–1937	SCHRÖDINGER 1887–1961	HEISENBERG 1901–1976	DIRAC 1902–1984
Ernest Rutherford was a fiery New Zealander who "split the atom." While working in England he proved that atoms are made from smaller parts, and he discovered that they contain a tiny solid center, which he called the nucleus. He was one of the first people to investigate radioactivity—work that laid the foundations of atomic physics.	Austrian physicist Erwin Schrödinger figured out the complex math needed to show how atoms and the particles within them can behave as waves. He is best known for a famous puzzle in which the bizarre quantum world inside an atom is magnified to everyday dimensions, causing a cat to be both dead and alive at the same time.	German physicist Werner Heisenberg helped to figure out the puzzling inner world of the atom. At 23 he developed his theory of quantum mechanics, which won him a Nobel Prize. He also discovered the strange "uncertainty principle," which says it's impossible to know both the location and speed of a subatomic particle at the same time.	The English scientist Paul Dirac helped develop theories to show that subatomic particles like the electron behave as waves. Dirac's work helped to advance quantum mechanics. He also showed that a negatively charged electron must have a positively charged twin, a positron. He shared the Nobel Prize for physics with Schrödinger in 1933.

GLOSSARY

Absolute zero the lowest temperature possible (–459°F or –273°C), when all atoms stop moving.

Acceleration how quickly an object speeds up, slows down, or changes direction.

Aerodynamics the study of how objects move through air.

Atom a tiny particle of matter, consisting of a central nucleus surrounded by one or more electrons.

Battery a device that can produce or store electricity.

Buoyancy a force that pushes upward on an object when it's surrounded by liquid or gas.

Celsius a temperature scale based on the freezing point (0°C) and boiling point (100°C) of water.

Center of gravity a point in an object where all its weight appears to be concentrated. You can balance a pencil halfway along its length because that's where its center of gravity is.

Charge (or electric charge) the amount that an object can feel an electric force. It takes two forms: negative and positive.

Circuit the path through which an electric current can flow.

Conduction the movement of heat, sound, or electricity through a substance.

Conductor a substance that transmits heat, sound, or electricity well.

Convection the transfer of heat through a fluid (liquid or gas) by moving currents.

Drag force of resistance an object experiences when it travels through a gas or liquid.

Elastic an object is elastic if it returns to its original size and shape after being stretched.

Electric current the flow of electric charge (usually in the form of electrons) through a circuit.

Electricity effects caused by the movement of electric charges.

Electromagnetic ray a form of energy that travels at very high speed and can act as either waves or particles. Light and radio waves are types of electromagnetic ray.

Electron one of the three main particles in an atom (with the proton and neutron). It has a negative charge.

Energy the ability to do work (*see* work).

Evaporation a change of state in which a liquid turns into a gas (vapor).

Fluid a substance that flows. Liquids and gases are fluids.

Force a push or a pull. Forces change the speed, direction, or shape of objects.

Freezing point the temperature at which a liquid changes into a solid.

Frequency the number of waves that pass by each second.

Friction a force that hinders motion when one surface moves over another.

Gamma rays a type of electromagnetic ray with a very short wavelength. Gamma rays are emitted by radioactive substances.

Gas a state of matter in which the particles are far apart and move about randomly and quickly.

Gravity a force of attraction between all objects. Earth's gravity keeps our feet on the ground and makes objects fall when we drop them.

Heat a form of energy caused by the random motion of atoms.

Inertia the tendency of an object to resist any change in its motion.

Infrared ray a type of electromagnetic ray with a longer wavelength than visible light. Infrared rays transmit heat.

Insulator a material that is poor at conducting heat, sound, or electricity.

Interference a disturbance produced when two or more waves (such as light or sound) collide.

Lift the upward force produced on a wing when it moves through the air.

Light a type of electromagnetic ray that our eyes can see. White light is a mixture of all the colors of the rainbow, which together make up the visible spectrum.

Liquid a state of matter between a solid and a gas, in which the particles can slide around but remain close together and attract one another.

Magnetic field the region around a magnet, where its forces act.

Magnetism the property of some materials, especially iron, to attract or repel similar materials.

Mass the amount of matter in an object, measured in grams, kilograms, or metric tons. On Earth, an object's mass gives it weight. In space, objects are weightless but still have mass.

Matter anything that has mass and occupies space.

Melting point the temperature at which a solid turns into a liquid.

Microwaves electromagnetic rays with a wavelength longer than that of infrared rays but shorter than that of most radio waves. Microwaves are sometimes said to be a type of radio wave.

Molecule a particle of matter made of two or more atoms strongly bonded together.

Momentum the tendency of an object to keep on moving, equal to its mass times its velocity.

Neutron one of the two main particles in the nucleus of an atom. It has no electric charge.

Nucleus the solid center of an atom, made up of protons and neutrons. It contains most of the atom's mass.

Particles basic units from which all substances are made, such as atoms or molecules. Subatomic particles are those smaller than an atom, such as protons.

Photon a particle of light or a particle of any other type of electromagnetic ray.

Physics the scientific study of force, motion, matter, and energy.

Potential energy energy stored for later use. Gravitational potential energy is the energy stored in an object because of its position, such as a roller coaster at the top of a hill.

Pressure how concentrated a force is over an area.

Prism a triangular wedge of glass or other transparent material that can split white light into a spectrum of colors.

Proton one of the two main particles found in the nucleus of atoms. It has a positive charge.

Quantum a single, tiny unit of energy. Electromagnetic rays consist of a stream of quanta called photons.

Quark one of the ultimate building blocks of all matter. Protons and neutrons are made of three quarks each.

Radiation energy traveling as electromagnetic rays (such as light). The various types of ray given off by radioactive substances are also called radiation.

Radioactivity high-speed particles or electromagnetic rays given off when atomic nuclei break down.

Refraction the bending of a beam of light as it passes from one substance to another, such as from air to water.

Sound a kind of wave that travels through air or other materials, caused by molecules being briefly squeezed together.

Spectrum a succession of electromagnetic rays arranged in order of their wavelength, from shortest to longest. A rainbow is a spectrum of visible light wavelengths.

Speed how fast an object is moving, calculated as distance divided by time.

Streamlining shaping an object so that it travels with the least resistance, or drag, through air or water.

String in string theory, strings are the ultimate building blocks of the universe. Particles are waves on the string.

Strong nuclear force the force that holds the nucleus of an atom together. It is felt only by protons and neutrons and, unlike gravity or magnetism, acts only over very short distances.

Subatomic particle a particle that is smaller than an atom, such as a proton, electron, or quark.

Surface tension a force that causes the surface of water to form a weak skin.

Temperature measure of how hot or cold something is.

Ultraviolet (UV) light invisible electromagnetic ray with a shorter wavelength than visible light. UV rays in sunlight can burn skin.

Velocity the speed and direction of an object.

Viscosity A measure of how thick or runny a liquid is.

Wavelength the distance between the crest of one wave and the next.

Weight the downward force of an object's mass due to Earth's gravity.

Work a measure of the amount of energy used when something happens, equal to force times distance.

X-rays Electromagnetic rays with wavelengths between those of gamma rays and ultraviolet rays. X-rays pass through most parts of the human body, but not bones or teeth.

Zero-G alternative term for weightlessness.

INDEX

Acknowledgments

Dorling Kindersley would like to thank the following people for help with this book:
Tory Gordon-Harris, Rose Horridge, Anthony Limerick, Carrie Love, Lorrie Mack, Lisa Magloff, Rob Nunn, Laura Roberts-Jensen, Penny Smith, Fleur Star, Sarah Stewart-Richardson, Likengkeng Thokoa.

DK would also like to thank the following for permission to reproduce their images (key: a=above, b=below, c=center, l=left, r=right, t=top, b/g=background):

Advantage CFD: 46-47b. Alamy Images: Bruce McGowan 66bc; Ian M Butterfield 37bl; Pat Behnke 12tl (Diamond); Robert Llewellyn 73bl; Doug Steley 66bl; TF1 33crb, 46bl; Transtock Inc. 46tl, 47crb; Stephen Vowles 41 (soldier), 94 (soldier). Ariel Motor Company: 47tr, 95br. Corbis: 30bl, 33cra, 49 (golf ball), 71tc; Theo Allofs/zefa 67cla; Bettmann 18crb, 24bl, 27bl, 40-41b, 42tc, 59bl; Tom Brakefield 31 (cheetah); Ralph A. Clevenger 69tr; Richard Cummins 39cr, 66-67b; Ronnen Eshel 2bl, 26bl; Eurofighter/Epa 42tl; Al Francekevich 39br; Patrik Giardino 22cr; Beat Glanzmann/zefa 78cl; Images.com 5cla, 20-21; JLP/Jose Luis Pelaez/zefa 3 (hand), 23tr (hand); Kurt Kormann/zefa 79tr; Matthias Kulka/zefa 34tl; Lester Lefkowitz 42-43; George D. Lepp 47br; LWA-Sharie Kennedy 29 (moped); David Madison/zefa 40cl; Tim McGuire 38c; Amos Nachoum 51cra; Yuriko Nakao/Reuters 49br; Richard T. Nowitz 23cl; Robert Recker/zefa 83tc; Reuters 29cb, 30cl, 35cr, 47tl, 47cra; Galen Rowell 64tr; Wolfram Schroll/zefa 39c; G. Schuster/zefa 48br; Daniel Smith/zefa 66tc; Josh Westrich/zefa 3 (trolley), 25tl. Deutsches Museum, München: 31 (helios). DK Images: Adidas 1 (trainer); The All England Lawn Tennis Club, Church Road, Wimbledon, London, David Handley 48 (tennis ball); Anglo-Australian Observatory 14t (b/g), 17tc (b/g), 22tl (b/g); Audiotel 1 (spanner); Bradbury Science Museum, Los Alamos 34bl, 55bc; British Airways 1 (Concorde); The British Museum 60b (silk); Duracell Ltd 58cla; Ermine Street Guard 8bc; Football Museum, Preston 45 (boots), 61b (shirt); Sean Hunter 2fcl, 16tl; Indianapolis Motor Speedway Foundation Inc 36cb; Judith Miller/Kitsch-N-Kaboodle 22tl (Yoda); NASA 1 (astronaut), 10tr, 18bl; National Maritime Museum, London 16cr,

91fbl; Natural History Museum, London 9tc, 19fcrb, 90 (feather); Stephen Oliver 1 (domino), 13cra, 25 (car), 36c, 48 (basketball), 49 (basketball), 52bl, 62-63, 63bc, 63bl, 92fbl; Renault 88-89t; The Science Museum, London 11bl, 12fbr, 19bl, 50-51 (nails), 58bl, 91fbr; James Stevenson/National Maritime Museum, London 15cr; Florida Center for Instructional Technology: 9br. Getty Images: Allsport Concepts 22cl; Iconica 68cl; The Image Bank 23cr, 23bl, 74bl, 83crb; Nordic Photos 31 (Caravan); Photographer's Choice 36tl, 48tl, 83fcrb; David Robbins 83fcrb; Stock Illustration Source 87tl; Stone 38br; Stone+ 58fcla; Taxi 1 (skydiver), 2tl, 40-41t, 74-75 (Sun), 85cla. Carrie Love: 8cra (b/g). Mary Evans Picture Library: 28bc. NASA: Marshall Space Flight Center 1 (Shuttle). Photolibrary: Photolibrary.Com (Australia) 17br; Foodpix 35tr, 53tl, 54bl, 70tc; Index Stock Imagery 5tl (b/g), 6-7 (b/g), 50bc. PunchStock: Corbis 17cr. Photo Scala, Florence: 16cra. Joe Schwartz/Joyrides: 32r. Science & Society Picture Library: Science Museum Pictorial 29bl. Science Photo Library: 10br, 10cla, 54br, 90fcla, 90cla, 90bl, 92fcla, 92cla; American Institute Of Physics 93fcra; David Becker 39bl; George Bernard 91cra; British Antarctic Survey 82crb; Dr. Jeremy Burgess 38tl, 80-81b; CERN 76br; John Chumack 85bl; Crawford Library/Royal Observatory, Edinburgh 15bc; Professor Harold Edgerton 45bc, 72-73t; Prof. Peter Fowler 93fcla; Mark Garlick 67br; Henry Groskinsky, Peter Arnold Inc. 48c; GUSTO 74tc; Roger Harris 15tr, 62tl; Keith Kent 31 (Thrust); Edward Kinsman 72c; Mehau Kulyk 5bl, 74tl; Laguna Design 88bl; Damien Lovegrove 74bc; Max-Planck-Institut/American Institute Of Physics 93cra; NASA 31 (Apollo15), 33bl; National Library Of Medicine 92cra; Claude Nuridsany & Marie Perennou 74br; David Parker 74-75, 79cla, 81cr (bubble); Pasieka 74-75b, 77tl; D. Phillips 52tc, 65tl; Philippe Plailly 52-53b, 54bc; D. Roberts 82clb; Royal Observatory, Edinburgh 18-19 (map); Erich Schrempp 80cr; Science, Industry & Business Library/New York Public Library 17tr; Dr. Gary Settles 44bl; Francis Simon/American Institute Of Physics 93cla; Sinclair Stammers 80tr, 81cl, 81cb; Takeshi Takahara 46cb; Ted Kinsman 83fclb; Sheila Terry 3 (Atlas), 14bl, 63fcra, 70clb, 79cb, 91fcla, 91cla, 91fcra; Gianni Tortoli 3 (heliocentric), 15cl; US Library Of Congress 35br, 86br, 92fcra; Detlev Van Ravenswaay 19cr, 90cra, 90br. Sky TV: from Sky One's Brainiac 70-71b. www.mclaren.com: 31 (McLaren).

All other images © Dorling Kindersley
For further information see:
www.dkimages.com